Pentecostal Potpourri

R Glenn Brown

ISBN: 061597371X
ISBN 13: 9780615973715

Table Of Contents

Foreward

Pentecostal Potpourri is a mixture of insightful articles relating to the Pentecostal doctrine of speaking in tongues. Glenn Brown, for fifty-two years an ordained minister with the Assemblies of God until he resigned in 2010, analyzes the traditional stance of American Pentecostalism from an insider's perspective. He describes clearly his doctrinal differences with his former church and decisively exegetes pertinent Scripture to support his position.

Brown has no quarrel with speaking in tongues. He recognizes that this is clearly one of the spiritual gifts bestowed by the Holy Spirit. However, he strongly believes that American Pentecostals have assigned an invalid purpose for tongues. He decries the disunity within Pentecostalism itself and the division it has produced within the Christian Church as a whole.

The author points out the errors American Pentecostals make in assigning tongues as initial required physical evidence of Spirit baptism. But more than that, he exegetes Old Testament scriptures (the only Bible available to the first Christians) that present a vastly superior purpose for tongues at Pentecost. Brown specified, *"American Pentecostals,"* since multitudes world-wide in the Pentecostal/Charismatic movement do not adhere to the doctrine that there is no valid Spirit baptism unless evidenced by speaking in tongues.

These sixteen essays deal almost exclusively with the erroneous purpose American Pentecostals assigned to the "tongues" that accompanied the outpouring of the Spirit at Pentecost and subsequently. Consequently, there is some repetition. If anyone finds the repetition objectionable the author will gladly refund the purchase price. However, each one sheds additional light on a particular issue connected to the central issue. If a reader comes across an essay that he or she would like to copy and send to someone, permission is granted.

Introduction

While doing scriptural and historical research for a book my mind is sometimes activated to pursue a certain theological idea to a reasonable and scriptural conclusion. *PENTECOSTAL POTPOURRI* is the result of ideas that came to mind while I was writing *Pentecost REVISITED* and *Pentecost REKINDLED.* As you read these essays you will discover that each has a common theme revolving around two subjects. One is the baptism in the Holy Spirit as the Spirit fell upon the early disciples at Pentecost (Acts 2:1-4). The other is the supernaturally inspired languages that accompanied the outpouring of the Spirit. These languages (tongues) were unknown to the speakers but clearly understood by the religious pilgrims gathered from across the Roman Empire (Acts 2:5-21).

American Pentecostalism, by and large, has declared that these appendages to Spirit baptism are absolutely necessary as physical evidence of valid baptism in the Holy Spirit. For more than fifty years I was associated with the Assemblies of God, a leading proponent of this doctrine. My pursuit of scriptural truth led me to the conviction that my church erred in its teaching about the purpose of the accompanying supernaturally spoken languages at Pentecost. I was encouraged to discover in my research that world-wide, multitudes of Pentecostals and Charismatics do not subscribe to the tradition prescribed by

American Pentecostalism. I am pained by the needless division my denomination has produced within Pentecostalism as well as in the Church in general.

I resigned from my church denomination in 2010 after writing *Pentecost REVISITED*. This book elicited numerous responses and questions, some of which are dealt with in these essays. Further study and research produced new insights that I wished I had included in my first book. I wrote a second entitled *Pentecost REKINDLED* which contains material from the first book but much new material as well. It is currently with a publisher and should be published in the spring of 2014, about the same time as *Pentecostal Potpourri*.

I will be forever grateful to the Assemblies of God officials in the Northern California/Nevada District who agave me warm fellowship and a covering for my ministry for forty years. This despite the knowledge that I differed with them about a key doctrine. I regret any pain that the public declaration of my stance may inflict. For forty years I remained publicly silent about my digression because I had not yet discovered the scriptural purpose for "evidential tongues". When I sensed I had uncovered a biblical truth that I had long overlooked, I could remain silent no longer. At my age, I am on the cusp of eternity. Before long I must give an account of how I have responded to the truth I believe God has revealed to me from His word. It is this awesome responsibility that compels me to write as I do.

You will discover that I do not quarrel with the legitimacy of the spiritual gift of "speaking in tongues". It is the purpose that American Pentecostals assign this gift that I strongly resist. I believe the "gifts of the Spirit" have been restored to the Church. Much of the Evangelical church rejected the truth about the restoration of spiritual gifts because they associated this with Pentecostalism's erroneous teaching about the purpose of tongues. The latter they clearly saw was not supported by Scripture. To the detriment of the western Church, the cessationists discarded the baby with the bath water, to use a descriptive but overworked phrase. Fortunately, the emerging Church is rediscovering the gifts of the Spirit in a powerful way and Cessationism (doctrine that the supernatural "gifts" have ceased) is on the wane. This subject is also covered in some length in my books. It is my prayer that these exegetical studies will prove a blessing to God's people.

R. Glenn Brown,
Sequim, Washington
February 16, 2014

one

LET ME EXPLAIN

As many of you may know, my understanding of the purpose of speaking in tongues, when it accompanies the baptism in the Holy Spirit, has undergone a transition over the past six decades. I was baptized in the Spirit in March 1948. Twenty years later, while serving as a U.S. Navy chaplain in Vietnam, I realized that I could no longer affirm my allegiance to the traditional Assemblies of God position that valid baptism in the Holy Spirit must always be accompanied by the initial physical evidence of speaking in tongues.

When I returned home in 1969 I obeyed my conscience and, with some fear and trepidation, indicated my variance on the annual questionnaire required for Assemblies of God ministers. I knew that this official acknowledgement could result in my dismissal from the denomination. Dismissal would mean that my ecclesiastical endorsement as a chaplain would be withdrawn and I could no longer serve in the ministry to which I believed God had called me. My conscience, under the probing of the Holy Spirit, compelled me to take that risk.

The District in which I was ordained, and to which I belonged at the time, did attempt to have me dismissed but, providentially,

I was invited to transfer to the Northern California/Nevada District. Joe Gerhart, the District Superintendent at the time, welcomed me with open arms. He assured me that his district would have no problem with my position. Upon retiring from the Navy I was requested by this District to serve as pastor of the Assemblies of God church in Pleasanton, CA where I ministered for nearly fourteen years.

Upon retiring from the pastorate, Donna and I sensed the call of God to minister in Eastern Europe. The collapse of the Soviet Union had opened many doors formerly closed to missionaries. In 1992, shortly after my retiring from the pastorate, a former Soviet officer serving as Commanding General of a huge Ukrainian military complex near the Hungarian and Slovakian borders, approached David Clark, an American missionary ministering near the General's headquarters.

This Ukrainian military commander had an unusual request. He wanted David to demonstrate to his Command how American military chaplains minister to our armed forces.The missionary confessed he had no military ministry experience and could not demonstrate how chaplains serve. However, he promised the general he would try to find a retired chaplain who would respond to his request. Through a series of providential events, in June 1993 I found myself sitting in General Zoblotny's office in Mukachevo, Ukraine accepting his invitation to return to Ukraine and demonstrate how American chaplains perform ministry to troops.

I returned to Pleasanton, sold our home there and got Donna relocated with our daughter in Seattle. By October I was ready to return to Ukraine and fulfill my promise to General Zoblotny. Before departing I met with the District Presbytery for their blessing. District Superintendent Don Annas wrote a letter designating me as the District liason for military ministry in E. Europe. To my knowledge, I was the first American chaplain (retired) invited to minister to former Soviet troops in independent Ukraine.

Now more than 20 years later, I can testify that God has been faithful. I have returned to Ukraine thirty-seven times, never missing a year in which I did not return and minister at least once and usually twice a year. The ministry has taken many twists and turns. After about three years the open door to military bases was closed to me. But there were now converted Ukrainian officers who could carry on ministry inside the military establishment.

Over the years God enabled Donna and me to help found churches, buy buildings, conduct and sponsor numerous conferences and establish an orphanage in Mukachevo, Ukraine. I ministered in Baptist churches as well as churches in the Pentecostal Union and the Charismatic Union. I have become friends with the Orthodox leader of ministry to Ukrainian military personnel and served with him in several conferences aimed at establishing a Ukrainian chaplaincy.

During more than fifty years of ordained ministry with the Assemblies of God I refrained from going public about my break with the denominational tradition. I limited any discussion of the matter to Assemblies of God officials, family members and a few close friends. There were several reasons for this decision to remain silent. (1) I was sure there was a genuine experience of being baptized in the Holy Spirit validated by scripture which was accompanied by the gift of tongues. (2) I was convinced that the Assemblies of God tradition regarding the purpose of tongues that accompanied Spirit baptism was in error because it had no solid scriptural foundation. I could clearly see that it was based on a series of assumptions and no "thus saith the Lord." I had seen how this tradition hindered the Holy Spirit from fulfilling Jesus' prayer for unity among his followers. I had seen how it helped foster a spiritual caste system similar to Corinth. (3) And of course, while I served an Assemblies of God church, I was ethically constrained to remain silent. (4) But the one thing always tugging at the back of my mind was this question: Since tongues were not meant to be the unique initial physical evidence of Spirit baptism what was their purpose? This drove me to a prayerful search of scripture. It would not be helpful to go public without a biblical response to this question.

Insert: Something long overlooked occurred to me. The only Bible the first disciples had was the Old Testament. That is where they must find the purpose for tongues at Pentecost.

The first pertinent Old Testament passage is Joel 2:28 as quoted by Peter in Acts 2:17; *"In the last days, God says, I will pour out my Spirit on all people. Your sons and daughters will prophesy, your young men will see visions, and your old men will dream dreams."* I want to point out an overlooked truth about Peter's sermon text. At the time he preached, Peter did not believe the first sentence of his text. He did not believe that God would pour out his Spirit on all people. He firmly believed it would happen only to Jewish believers and proselytes who submitted to Jewish ordinances. This is fully and dramatically attested to in Acts 10.

How could the Holy Spirit be poured out on all people if Peter, Jesus' chief lieutenant on earth, was convinced only believing Jews and converts to Judaism were welcome into the Messiah's kingdom? It was impossible. How could Jesus defuse this crisis? Jesus' answer was simple. Peter's bondage to his ancient tradition concerning Jews had to be broken. Peter must be freed from his attitude of racism before the gospel could penetrate to "the ends of the earth." The employment of tongues accompanying Spirit baptism figured large in Christ's plan as we shall see.

The other Old Testament passage is the one Paul quoted loosely from Isaiah 28:11-12 in First Corinthians 14:21; *"In the law it is written: 'Through men of strange tongues and through the lips of foreigners I will speak to this people, but even then they will not listen to me,' says the Lord."* From this Isaiah passage Paul extracts this principle; *"Tongues, then, are a sign, not for believers, but for unbelievers.* "v.22a The conjunction "then" clearly refers back to the Old Testament passage. Grammatically, the conjunction will allow no other conclusion.

So what does that mean as it relates to the interpretation of this passage? Obviously, Paul must see a parallel relationship between God's Old Testament chosen people in captivity who "will not listen" to the sign of tongues and his chosen people in the NT who fail to understand the sign of tongues. In both cases, it is God's chosen people who have closed their ears to the sign of tongues. The Isaiah passage makes clear that the unbelievers are disobedient Jews

Let's look closely at the Isaiah passage. Who are the "men of strange tongues" who are speaking? The context reveals that these are the Assyrian conquerors of Israel. Who is "this people...who will not listen?" They are God's chosen people, Israelites, about to be carried into Assyrian captivity because of disobedience and unbelief. Moses and the prophets had warned

Israel what would happen if she disregarded God's commands. The strange language of the Assyrian captors was a constant sign to these unbelieving Israelites that God had kept his word. When Paul considers tongues generically, as they were initially evidenced at Pentecost and later at Caesarea, he draws the conclusion voiced in verse 22 quoted above.

When we apply Paul's principle to the generic outpourings of the Spirit we discover how beautifully it applies. Consider the outpouring at Pentecost. The Holy Spirit was poured out upon the waiting 120 just as Jesus had promised. The Spirit manifested himself with tongues like fire dancing over the head of each, just as John the Baptist had predicted. This was the sign that confirmed the arrival of the Spirit. There was nothing said by Jesus or the Baptist that would lead them to think that speaking in tongues was a sign or evidence that they had been baptized in the Holy Spirit. Nevertheless, they did speak in other tongues (languages) *"as the Spirit enabled them."* So what was the purpose of this phenomenon? If it was not a sign for the disciples for whom was it a sign? The principle Paul derived from Isaiah 28:11-12 applies here. Tongues were a sign to unbelievers. And who were the unbelievers? They were the thousands of God's chosen people (Jews) who had gathered in Jerusalem from all over the Roman Empire to celebrate the feast of Pentecost.

They refused to believe the messianic prophecies and rejected Jesus as their Messiah. It was as a supernatural sign for these thousands of unbelieving celebrants of Pentecost. And the tongues accomplished their purpose. The Jewish pilgrims were astonished and curious. They began to ask questions, providing Simon Peter with the opportunity to preach his first Spirit empowered sermon. His prophetic message resulted in three thousand unbelievers becoming believers in Jesus as their Messiah. Did not Paul say that prophecy (anointed preaching) would convict the unbeliever of sin and lead him to worship God?

As I mentioned above, Peter did not really believe or accept as true all of the text from which he preached when the Spirit was outpoured at Pentecost. His tradition had so "brainwashed" him that he dared not even consider another view. (Tradition has a way of doing that.) He was absolutely convinced that only Jews or proselytes (Gentiles who had submitted to Jewish ordinances) could be saved. Yes, his sermon text from Joel said, *"I will pour out my Spirit on all people"* but Peter could not accept the little word "all." This mind-set persisted despite Joel's declaration and three years of exposure to the teaching of Jesus.

And speaking of exposure to the teaching and example of Jesus, consider the encounter Jesus had with the Roman centurion recorded in Luke 7:1-10. Peter was present when Jesus ministered to the centurion and healed his servant. He surely heard Jesus' surprising (to Peter) declaration, *"I tell you, I have not found such great faith even in Israel."* Peter heard the words but they never altered his racist attitude.

Not only did this attitude persist in Peter but it prevailed among all the Jewish believers. How was the gospel to penetrate the Gentile world when the proclaimers were racist to the core? It would never happen unless radical changes were made in the hearts and minds of Jewish Christians and it must start with Peter. How was Jesus to accomplish this transformation if three years of his teaching and his example had failed to do so?

Jesus had a plan and "tongues" played a major role in it. To break the strangle-hold that prejudice had on Peter, God orchestrated a strange series of events. First, there was the large screen dramatic presentation on the house top in Joppa.

Peter was compelled to rethink his ideas about what was clean and unclean. Then there was the clear-cut command for him to not quibble about going to Caesarea with the requesting Gentile delegation dispatched by Captain Cornelius, the Roman centurion. But the strangest and most dramatic events took place in Cornelius' house. His family, plus trusted soldiers and servants, were all gathered to hear what Peter had to say. They were listening raptly as Peter began to share the gospel story. Suddenly Peter was interrupted by strange and totally unexpected sounds from his Gentile audience. They were praising God and speaking in other tongues just like the disciples had done at Pentecost.

Peter and the Jewish Christians who had accompanied him from Joppa were astounded, surprised, flabbergasted...there is no word too strong to describe their reaction to what they heard. How could it be that these uncircumcised, crude Gentile interlopers could have received the baptism in the Holy Spirit with the sign of other tongues just as the disciples had at Pentecost? And for whom was the sign intended? Not for the Gentiles. They had received no teaching about the Holy Spirit. They had not even heard one complete sermon. They had not been baptized in water. They had no anticipation of speaking in tongues and it had no meaning for them other than a supernatural expression of praise.

Tongues were clearly a sign to the unbelievers. And who were the unbelievers? Why prejudiced Peter and his equally prejudiced companions, of course. Peter had discounted the prophet Joel and the teaching and example of Jesus. But, thank God, he deciphered the supernatural sign of tongues. This tradition-bound leader got the message and exclaimed to his bewildered companions, *"Can anyone keep these people from being baptized with water? They have received the Holy Spirit just as we have."* Acts 10:47

Seeing Pentecostal tongues from its scriptural perspective was a gloriously liberating experience for me.

> I must admit, it was a gloriously freeing experience for me to see tongues in this light. For forty years I had been burdened with the conviction that speaking in tongues was not the unique initial physical evidence of being baptized in the Holy Spirit but could give no positive purpose for tongues accompanying Spirit baptism. Now I saw all the pertinent Old Testament and New Testament scriptures fit together harmoniously. Speaking in tongues was God's sign that the division and disunity caused by "strange tongues" at Babel could be reversed. How can this reversal occur? It can happen only when God's people recognize that His Spirit has been outpoured in order to free us from every tradition, every cultural mind-set, every selfish attitude that leads to disunity among followers of Jesus Christ. The "unknown tongues" symbolize all the languages of the world which the gospel will unite in Jesus Christ.

Good friends of mine have expressed concern that my going public with my convictions will cause division within the Assemblies of God. I have been scolded with brotherly concern, "Glenn, your teaching about unity within the body of Christ will be undermined by creating disunity within the Assemblies of God." My goal is not to create disunity within the church I served for more than half a century. Disunity already exists. Many leaders give lip service to our traditional doctrine but hesitate to proclaim it because they struggle with the same doubts I did. Churches even change their names so as not to be identified as

Assemblies of God. This despite the denomination's attempt to have every member church publicly display its affiliation.

Unity within a denomination built upon a tradition that is not clearly and specifically taught in Scripture will inevitably promote division within the body of Christ. Eventually disunity will erupt within the denomination itself. It may take decades before unifying biblical truth replaces imbedded divisive tradition. Martin Luther can attest to that in his struggle with his own church. The Holy Spirit will never cease working in the hearts of Christians to bring about the fulfillment of Christ's prayer; *"That they may be one as we are one: I in them and you in me. May they be brought to complete unity to let the world know that you have sent me and have loved them even as you have loved me."* John 17:22b-23.

Another lament from a close friend steeped in traditional Pentecostalism needs to be confronted. He fears that my understanding of scripture, if it becomes widely accepted, will discourage people from seeking to be baptized in the Spirit. I believe this is an irrational fear, perhaps motivated by an unconscious desire to retain control of how to assess Spirit baptism. Jesus is the sovereign baptizer in the Holy Spirit. Once he is released from the traditional box in which we have tried to imprison him I believe many more people will be candidates for Spirit baptism.

On what do I base this conclusion? First, as world conditions deteriorate and the forces of evil become more pronounced, Christians will become increasingly thirsty for the anointing and power of the Holy Spirit. We see this now, particularly third world countries in Africa, Asia and S. America. Second, when the experience of being baptized in the Holy Spirit is no longer irrevocably tied to a physical evidence that can be counterfeited, abused and misused then sincere believers will trust

Christ to baptize them as he sovereignly chooses. When Jesus baptizes in the Spirit the recipient will know when it happens. Soon others will know it as well. There will be a fresh anointing of spiritual power. This anointing will manifest itself in gifting for service and in character traits that reflect the nature of Jesus Christ. The gifts and fruit of the Spirit ministered in power and love display the Holy Spirit in His fullness.

In conclusion, let me reflect back forty years. At that time I had no insight as to the purpose of tongues that accompanied Spirit baptism. However, I was convinced there was no scriptural foundation for the assertion that Jesus Christ (the **B**aptizer) must authenticate every one he baptized in the Spirit with the initial physical evidence of speaking in tongues. Even if all the Spirit baptisms recorded in scripture were accompanied by tongues I knew it would be arrogant of me to insist my sovereign Lord could not baptize in any fashion he chose. The only criteria that he must fulfill were self-imposed. The baptism in the Holy Spirit must entail an impartation of spiritual power and the ability to bear witness to people everywhere concerning the risen Christ. (Acts 1:8)

It is not immediately apparent that only half of Jesus' promise concerning Spirit baptism was fulfilled at Pentecost. They all received an impartation of power. What is often overlooked is that Pentecost did not equip the 120 to be witnesses *"to the ends of the earth."* All these Jewish followers of Jesus were still completely bound by their ancient Jewish tradition. They did not believe Gentiles could be part of the Christian community without submitting to the rites of Judaism (become proselytes).

The outpouring of the Holy Spirit at Azusa Street in 1906 is a significant historical occasion. A largely black congregation led by a pastor whose parents had been slaves suddenly became the focus of the religious world. Blacks and whites, ministers and laymen and curious onlookers of all colors and backgrounds gathered to see what was going on. Los Angeles now joined Jerusalem, Caesarea and Ephesus as a site where the Holy Spirit had been outpoured accompanied by speaking in tongues. The secular press had a field day ridiculing the strange phenomena that accompanied this Divine visitation. It was essentially the same response Paul describes when unbelievers heard Christian worshippers speaking tongues en masse in Corinth. "These people are crazy."

We should not be surprised that the secular world misunderstood what was taking place at Azusa Street in Los Angeles. The press played up the spectacular because it sold papers. But they had absolutely no insight about supernatural manifestations of the Holy Spirit. A far greater tragedy is that the Christian world misunderstood what God was doing at Azusa Street. In a fashion nearly as dramatic as the outpouring on the Gentiles at Caesarea, God poured out his Spirit upon black Americans. They were a people only a generation out of slavery, still economically deprived, forced to accept second-class citizenship and endure the humiliation which accompanied their status.

Azusa Street was God's sign to unbelievers. No, not to unbelievers in the pagan secular world. It was a sign to unbelieving white Christians in America and around the world. What did they not believe? They did not believe that blacks were fully equal to whites. They did not believe blacks should be fully integrated into American society and into the family of God. We white Christians were as bound by tradition and prejudice against blacks as Simon Peter and the early Jewish Christians were against Gentiles. I am not pointing fingers. If I had been present then I would likely have done the same although it pains me to acknowledge this.

Jesus used the same supernatural sign at Azusa Street as he had at Caesarea to break the wall of partition between people groups. The sign was an unexpected and mighty outpouring of the Holy Spirit accompanied by tongues upon a largely black congregation. Congregations in many places had been praying for God to pour out his Spirit again as he had on the apostolic church. Many of these spiritually thirsty people flocked to Los Angeles to see what was happening. Those with hungry and receptive hearts were filled with the Spirit and spoke in tongues. There was a wonderful spirit of love and acceptance among the diverse racial groups that gathered. For a short time, God's people seemed to understand the sign of tongues? Was the prayer of Jesus for unity among his followers at last going to be answered? Unfortunately, the positive response to the sign of tongues was short lived.

Before three years had passed a divisive spirit shattered the love and harmony that initially prevailed. The sign not only was rejected; it was so altered it became unrecognizable. The tongues of Azusa were Christ's sign that blacks were to be accepted into the Christian community without prejudice. The sign was not believed. The scourge of racism continued, nurtured and encouraged by Charles Parham and those who followed in his train. He was the talented Pentecostal preacher who first insisted that tongues must accompany Spirit baptism or it was invalid. The sign designed to produce unity was transformed into a sign that fostered division. How did this happen? The fascination with the spectacular was more attractive than the inner character change the supernatural sign pointed to. Decades of racial strife resulted. God had to use the power of government to enforce changes that the body of Christ should have voluntarily initiated and promoted.

Some readers have difficulty with my use of the term "unbelievers." The bible speaks of two kinds of unbelievers. (1) There are unbelievers who reject Jesus Christ and any claim He has upon their lives. Many do not even believe in God. Many are avowed secular materialists. Examples are reflected in coverage of Azusa Street by secular reporters. The Corinthian unbelievers may be in this category. (2) There are Christian "unbelievers" in the sense that followers of Jesus may fail to grasp an essential truth and thus believe an error or grasp a truth but fail to embrace it. We see examples of this in Matthew 16:21-23 and Hebrews 3:12. In the Old Testament this would also include the Jews, God's chosen people. It particularly includes the Israelites referred to in I Corinthians 14:21 from Isaiah 28:11-12.

In I Corinthians 14:22-23 we have an unusual situation. "Unbelievers" in verse 22 clearly refers back to the captive Israelites mentioned in verse 21. These are God's chosen people who have failed to embrace God's revealed truth. The "other tongues" were intended as a sign to these unbelieving Israelites who have failed to embrace prophetic truth. From this Old Testament example Paul is apparently using "tongues" in a generic sense. Here and in Acts 2:17, 21 are the only places in Scripture that teach concerning the purpose of tongues as manifested at Pentecost and subsequently. When we apply Paul's principle to the Spirit baptisms on Jews in Jerusalem (Pentecost) and in Caesarea (Gentiles) we see how it is confirmed.

The unbelievers at Pentecost were the thousands of Jews (God's chosen people under the Old Covenant) who heard their native languages being spoken by ignorant Galilean peasants.

The sign of tongues captured their immediate attention and provided an opportunity for Peter to preach his powerful sermon. However, it was Peter's prophetic preaching that led to repentance from sin and belief in Jesus as Messiah. Isn't that exactly what Paul depicts in first Corinthians 14?

The unbelievers at Caesarea were Simon Peter and his Jewish companions from Joppa. The tongues accompanying the Gentile's Spirit baptism was the sign that convinced Peter and the other Jewish Christians that Gentiles were to be accepted into the church without undergoing Jewish rites.

The Corinthian unbelievers in verse 23 in all probability are curious pagan Gentiles who have not yet come to faith in Christ. Tongues as practiced en masse in the Corinthian church did not function as a sign to these pagan unbelievers. Rather, this manifestation led to the conclusion that the "tongue speakers" were insane. Admittedly, I Corinthians 14:20-23 is a very difficult passage to exegete. As I have pointed out elsewhere, J.B. Phillips, renowned Bible translator, despaired of making sense of it. He appended a note with this admission; "This is the sole instance of the translator's departing from the accepted text. He felt bound to conclude from the sense of the next three verses, that we have here either a slip of the pen on the part of Paul, or, more probably, a copyist's error." Gordon Fee makes an equally serious error. Fee discounts the significance of the Old Testament quote and thus misses the thrust of Paul's thinking.

The Isaiah quotation is actually the key to the whole passage. Otherwise, why did Paul quote it, prefaced by the exhortation; *"Brothers, stop thinking like children. In regard to evil be infants, but in your thinking be adults."* v. 20. In other words, "Put your thinking caps on. Don't continue in your misunderstanding of the purpose of the miraculous languages displayed at Pentecost." I believe the explanation I have suggested is consistent with the immediate context and with the larger Old Testament and New Testament contexts. I have seen no exegetical study that takes these larger contexts into consideration though there may well be. If you come to this passage with a firm commitment to a doctrinal tradition you will probably seek another explanation. There are many available. Choose one and then compare with the one I have asked you to consider. May the Lord grant us spiritual perception so that we can distinguish scriptural truth from human tradition.

two

WHOM DO YOU TRUST?

The Assemblies of God, and other Pentecostal denominations, have gifted, charismatic leaders who exert great influence in their respective spheres of activity. They are highly respected and honored for their ministry gifts. They are in great demand as speakers, teachers, and conference leaders. People in their sphere of influence may conclude: "Surely I can trust the teaching of these respected leaders regarding the purpose of tongues that accompany Spirit baptism. I know their lives and history. They are good men (or women). I am sure they would not lead me astray. If I can't trust them whom can I trust?"

I can relate to these thoughts. I have greatly admired and respected Assemblies of God leaders whom I knew during my years as a Navy chaplain and later as a pastor. Donna and I have entertained in our home men like C.M. Ward and General Superintendent Thomas Zimmerman. Assistant General Superintendent Bert Webb was a dear friend and brother in Christ and wonderful supporter of Assemblies of God chaplains. These men will only be historical footnotes to younger Assemblies of God adherents but they were once household names in the Assemblies of God family circle. I could refer to dear friends like Joe Gerhart and others who followed him as

District Superintendents of the Northern California/Nevada District, some still living and active. I am honored and humbled to have had their friendship and support. But great men, filled with the Holy Spirit, marvelous and successful preachers with godly reputations can be mistaken. I will demonstrate this by an example from scripture.

There was a powerful leader in the Apostolic church. Jesus had promoted him to be first among equals in the apostolic circle. He was part of the inner ring of three that Jesus entrusted to accompany him at His transfiguration on the mount and later his agony in the garden. He was the Apostolic spokesman anointed to preach to the curious and questioning throng of Jewish pilgrims celebrating Pentecost. His text was from Joel 2:28-32. He was a gifted preacher and three thousand responded to his Spirit anointed sermon and acknowledged Jesus as their Savior and Messiah (Acts 2:40-41). I have read this account in the second chapter of Acts many, many times. Only recently did something very significant about this passage reach out and grab me. Here's the truth the Holy Spirit seared into my mind and heart: *PETER DID NOT BELIEVE NOR PRACTICE THE TEXT WHICH HE QUOTED FROM JOEL.*

Peter was no hypocrite. He was a good man who would never deliberately lead anyone astray. But unfortunately, he was bound by a powerful religious tradition that kept him blinded to the truth at the heart of the very text he quoted. Let's examine the biblical data. Look carefully at the opening statement of the text, *"In the last days, God says, I will pour out my Spirit on ALL PEOPLE."* (Acts 2:17) Now observe the last statement of the text, *"And EVERONE who calls on the name of the Lord will be saved."* (Acts 2:21) These verses from Joel clearly depict a universal outpouring of the Spirit and salvation for all who call on the Lord

Peter clearly missed the purpose of tongues at Pentecost. He was fully convinced, as were the other disciples, that only Jews and proselytes (i.e. Gentiles who converted to Judaism) could receive the Spirit or be saved. But they were wrong. Peter's enlightenment became the catalyst that produced freedom for multitudes of other Jewish Christians bound by the same tradition.

The climax of Peter's emancipation came eight years later when Jesus sovereignly poured out the Spirit upon crude, and often despised, soldiers at the Roman army garrison in Caesarea. Without apostolic sanction, without any instruction, without any preconceived idea of purpose, these uncouth Gentiles began to praise God in languages supernaturally uttered. Peter at last understood the meaning of the text from Joel. Tongues were the divine sign that every language group, race or nation was welcome to receive the Holy Spirit and salvation. There were no people groups unclean or unacceptable

God help Assemblies of God leaders not to continue to perpetuate the error of Peter and thereby overlook or deny the unifying purpose of tongues. Where is the leader who will be the catalyst to bring needed change to our divisive tradition?

We Pentecostals have taught that when tongues accompany Spirit baptism it indicates that we have totally surrendered to Jesus Christ. This is based on Jame's statement that the tongue is the most unruly member of the body and (it is assumed) if it is surrendered all has been surrendered. Peter had certainly been baptized in the Holy Spirit. Unquestionably, he had spoken in tongues. But everything had not been surrendered.

Despite the command of Jesus that the gospel must be preached to all nations, despite Joel's clear declarations of the universality of the gospel, Peter held tenaciously to his biased Jewish tradition. It took a series of miracles and stern commands from heaven before the tentacles of this egoistic, obsessive tradition were broken. If a great Spirit-filled Pentecostal leader like the Apostle Peter was victimized by his religious tradition isn't it possible that other Pentecostal leaders have fallen into the same trap? The only source for trustworthy Christian doctrine is the whole counsel of inspired Scripture.

three

THE MAN WITHOUT A CHURCH

I can relate to Edward Everett Hale's classic short story, *"The Man Without a Country."* Hale apparently wrote this fictional account as an allegory promoting the Union cause during the Civil War. His book exerted a powerful influence for prioritizing national unity over the interests of individual states.

I have recently written a book (*Pentecost REVISITED*) promoting unity within the body of Christ which conflicts with one of the hallowed traditions of my church. As a result I have become *"The Man Without a Church."* Here's how it happened. For more than half a century I enjoyed ecclesiastical endorsement as an ordained minister with the General Council of the Assemblies of God. Forty years ago while serving as a U. S. Navy chaplain I risked losing my chaplaincy ministry by declaring that I could no longer affirm the denominational creed relating to speaking in tongues. The position of my church is that there is no valid baptism in the Holy Spirit unless it is initially physically evidenced by speaking in tongues. I could find no solid scriptural evidence for this position and said so on my annual questionnaire required for credential renewal. As a result the officials of my home District (Rocky Mountain) called for my dismissal.

The decision I made was not an easy one. I had grown up in an Assemblies of God preacher's home. My dad was a pastor and had served for several years as an Assistant District Superintendent and General Presbyter. Pentecostal tradition and doctrine had been drilled into my mind from early childhood. This, as well as the risk of being dismissed from the Navy chaplaincy, added to my mental and emotional turmoil. Nevertheless, my conscience and intellectual honesty compelled me to state my demurral.

Fortunately, my District officials did not have the authority to withdraw my ecclesiastical endorsement. They could only recommend this be done. The power to dismiss an ordained minister resided with the General Council at national Headquarters. The national office decided to extend my credentials another year so I could reconsider my position. Since my District was determined to have me released I knew that in another year I would again be facing dismissal. What could I do but pray and leave it in God's hands?

Providentially, Colonel John Lindval, a senior U.S. Army chaplain friend, recommended I talk to the Superintendent of the Northern California/Nevada District with which he was affiliated. I met with Superintendent Joe Gerhart and explained my situation. His response was more than I had hoped for: "Chaplain, transfer into my District. We will have no problem with your position." I made the transfer and for forty years (1970-2010) I enjoyed warm fellowship within the Northern California/Nevada District.

After retiring from the Navy with twenty-six years of military service I served as pastor of an Assemblies of God church in Pleasanton, California for nearly fourteen years. While pastor my dissent was limited to denominational officials and was never shared with the congregation. I retired from the pastorate in November 1991 just as the Soviet Union was imploding. Through another providentially ordered series of events, in June 1993 I was invited by a senior General in western Ukraine to minister to his military personnel in Transcarpatia. Thus began a ministry in Ukraine that continues to the present.

Although I could find no scriptural basis for the Pentecostal tradition that tongues must accompany every valid baptism in the Holy Spirit I knew tongues did accompany Spirit baptism at Jerusalem (Pentecost), Caesarea, and Ephesus. Pentecostals assumed the purpose was to signify a valid baptism in the Spirit. I eventually came to see this as a presumptuous assumption that clearly contradicted the plain statement of Joel as quoted by Peter. Furthermore, this assumption denied the Baptizer, Jesus, His sovereignty to baptize as He willed.

Making tongues the *sine qua non* proof of valid Spirit baptism opened the door to multiple aberrations.

Tongues can be counterfeited, misused and abused. They can and have led to a spiritual caste system. Christians who haven't spoken in tongues are regarded as second class citizens in some Pentecostal churches. Sincere, persistent seekers who do not receive the *evidence* of tongues become discouraged and even depressed. Some Pentecostals relegate speaking in tongues to a mechanical process and actually teach how to manipulate the tongue and lips so as to assist the Baptizer provide the required *evidence*. This gift may be, and too often has been, elevated above the Giver. Although critics have exaggerated these aberrations beyond their actual occurrence they exist and have helped create a gulf between Pentecostals and other Evangelicals. Would our Lord have ordained such a divisive purpose for tongues that countermands his own earnest, "death bed" request to His Father?

It is this lack of unity within the body of Christ that is of great concern to me. The knowledge that the iron-clad tradition of the church I was associated with for more than fifty years has contributed to the disunity compels me to write as I do. My research has convinced me that my church is out of step with much of the world-wide Pentecostal/Charismatic community. Dr. Allen Anderson, Professor of Global Pentecostal Studies at Birmingham University (England) has his finger on the international Pentecostal/Charismatic movement. He states, "Pentecostalism has taken on many forms quite different from those of North America and in a global context the North American types are not really meaningful...Many Pentecostal groups, including some of the largest Pentecostal churches in Europe and Latin America and many in the so-called Charismatic Movement, do not insist in the "initial evidence" of tongues." (Allen Anderson, *The Origin, Growth and Significance of the Pentecostal movements in the Third World,* Paper read at Post Graduate Seminar, Leeds University, Nov. 1977).

Despite its divisiveness and lack of a solid scriptural basis, why does American Pentecostalism so adamantly insist that Spirit baptism is valid only if initially evidenced by tongues? Frankly, one very cogent reason and perhaps the most compelling, is the personal experience of many Pentecostal believers. Although multitudes of Assemblies of God members have never spoken in tongues, many have. The experience of the vast majority of these is genuine and indicative of the Holy Spirit's activity. They assume that since tongues accompanied their experience of Spirit baptism the purpose of tongues must be to give evidence that their baptism is valid.

There is no doubt that tongues accompany many Spirit baptisms. This was certainly true of my own baptism in the Spirit. I assumed the tradition of my church was true and that I had received the necessary evidence of Spirit baptism. As a result of my indoctrination I neither knew nor sought any other explanation. It never occurred to me to seriously examine the Bible to see if our tradition had a solid scriptural foundation. For twenty years I continued to adhere loyally to the Pentecostal tradition in which I had been reared. During these twenty years I matured intellectually and spiritually. I developed a deep hunger for truth regardless of where it might lead.

I graduated from an Evangelical seminary where I had ardently defended my Pentecostal tradition. In 1960 I entered the U.S. Navy Chaplains' Corps. Here I served with godly men from other traditions. In defending my own tradition, more to myself than others, I discovered that our tradition was built on a series of assumptions without a clear biblical foundation. The major assumption was this: *Since three of the outpourings of the Spirit recorded in Acts were accompanied by speaking in tongues, we MUST assume that every valid Spirit baptism must be accompanied by tongues.*

No one that I know ever asked the question, "Could there possibly be a less divisive purpose for the tongues that accompany Spirit baptism?" Since the question was not asked an answer was not pursued. And millions accept the assumption, which fragmentizes the body of Christ, and claim it to be a biblical doctrine. When I ask, "Will you show me the scripture that undergirds your tradition?" They point to the outpourings of the Spirit in Jerusalem (Pentecost), Caesarea (Roman soldiers), and Ephesus (Asian Gentiles). Each is a different people group. What happened on these occasions is obvious. Those baptized in the Spirit spoke in tongues. But the purpose was not to give evidence of Spirit baptism. Tongues, as Joel testifies, signified, in a dramatic way, that all languages, all nations, all races, and all people groups are welcome into the kingdom of God.

When the thousands of pilgrims celebrating Pentecost asked what was the meaning of the tongues spoken supernaturally by the Galileans, Peter's inspired answer was to quote the prophet Joel, *"This (tongues) is that which was spoken by the prophet Joel, 'In the last days, God says, I will pour out my Spirit upon all flesh'"* (humanity). Joel's emphasis is not upon the outpouring of the Spirit. Many over the course of Israel's history had experienced that, including Joel himself. His emphasis is upon the universality of the outpouring in the "last days." The various languages are our Lord's reminder that there has been a major change in the divine economy. Joel clearly depicts this although Peter's allegiance to his old tradition prevented him from grasping it immediately. But after the visions at Joppa and the surprising outpouring of the Spirit on the Roman garrison in Caesarea, Peter began to understand the significance of Joel's inspired words. The various tongues are indeed a dramatic representation of "all humanity".

Fear is another reason why Pentecostals cling to their tradition. Pentecostals are hesitant to reexamine scripture and history lest they might discover a refutation of their hallowed tradition. My observation regarding theological training within American Pentecostal institutions is that they are schools of indoctrination rather than centers dedicated to a search for scriptural truth. There is no question that tongues accompanied Spirit baptisms in Jerusalem, Caesarea and Ephesus. This may have been true for Samaria and Damascus as well. But even if all five instances were accompanied by tongues it does not validate the conclusion reached by Charles Parham and his contemporaries at the dawn of the twentieth century... *Every valid Spirit baptism must be initially evidenced by speaking in tongues.* They were apparently so enamored with their supernatural experience that they never asked this crucial question: *Does scripture reveal another more important purpose for tongues that is firmly based on a biblical foundation?* Had they done so they would have discovered that Peter's sermon text from Joel gives a clear answer even though Peter at the time did not understand or except it.

I committed my life to Jesus Christ as a young soldier more than sixty years ago. I told Jesus that I could not possibly serve him unless he baptized me in the Holy Spirit and provided the power he had promised to his followers. Jesus and I had a dynamic dialogue in which He confronted me with issues that had to be resolved. When we had resolved the issues and my commitment was clear of any reservations He poured His Spirit upon me. This experience culminated in me worshipping the Lord in a language the Spirit provided.

Because of years of indoctrination in the Assemblies of God tradition I assumed that speaking in tongues was the evidential proof that I had been baptized in the Spirit. I was grateful for the experience and I have never doubted the reality of the gift of tongues. However, I knew deep in my heart that the proof of baptism in the Spirit for me personally was spiritual power, not tongues. Power was what Jesus had promised and what I sought and what I received.

Tongues were a sign that a revolutionary change had been introduced. They signaled that the Old Testament covenant of Mosaic law and works had been superseded by the New Testament covenant of grace and faith through the Messiah Jesus Christ. The Spirit had broken through the national boundary of Judaism. Salvation was now universally available. Tongues that accompanied Spirit baptism were our Lord's signal that the gospel now has universal application. It is the Spirit's proclamation that every language group, every race, every nationality and culture are equally welcome to become members of God's family.

Nothing restrains racism like the gospel

What if this unifying purpose for tongues had been acknowledged and proclaimed in 1906 following the Azusa Street outpouring? The ingrained racism that characterized American culture would likely have been restrained by black and white Spirit empowered Christians, united in Christ and with one another. Racism may not have been eliminated but there would have been a powerful Christian force of love and acceptance to help counter it. What if it had been acted upon following the outpouring of the Spirit in South Africa in 1908? But it wasn't. Disciples of Parham, himself a racist, were largely responsible for bringing Pentecostalism to South Africa.

Dr. Nico Horn, native of South Africa, and renowned for his coverage of Pentecostalism in his native land, offers this revealing observation:

"The Pentecostal outpouring of the Spirit in South Africa was no different from the outpouring in the United States. Racism in the Pentecostal movement in South Africa is not restricted to the apartheid era (i.e. after 1948...) Only six months after the initial

outpouring of the Holy Spirit in 1908, the executive council of the Apostolic Faith Mission (AFM) decided 'that the baptism of natives shall in future take place after the baptism of whites. From then onwards the Apostolic Faith Mission, the biggest and oldest Pentecostal movement in South Africa, moved towards separate congregations for white and black." (From an article entitled, CROSSING RACIAL BORDERS IN SOUTHERN AFRICA, June, 1991)

Would this spirit of racism in South Africa (which culminated in the evils of apartheid) erupted if Joel had been taken seriously? David Du Plessis, influential leader in the Apostolic Faith Mission, expressed remorse that his cooperation with the South African government had contributed to the government's implementation of apartheid. I knew David and greatly admired him. He was a great international ambassador for Pentecostals. I think his support of Apostolic Faith Mission's support of racism was one of the regrets of his life.

Pentecostals insist that tongues must accompany every valid Spirit baptism because their distinctive identity is hinged to this tradition. Tradition is more difficult to break than doctrine. Why is this true? For Evangelical Christians doctrine (hopefully) must be based on the clear teaching of scripture. If there is disagreement about a particular doctrine there is a common agreed upon authority that can be researched and investigated.

This is not true of tradition. It is based upon experiences (or lack thereof), dogmatic assertions by influential leaders, anecdotal illustrations and assumptions based largely on isolated texts divorced from the whole context of Scripture. This is true both of traditional Pentecostal teaching on tongues and the cessationist's tradition that tongues ended when the apostles died or when the canon of Scripture was sealed. When tradition is adopted as a "fundamental truth" this "distinctive" must be protected at all costs. The egos of those in leadership are heavily involved so that any threat to the tradition is taken as a personal threat.

four

THIS IS THAT

One of the favorite scripture passages for preachers when I was growing up in an Assemblies of God parsonage was Acts 2:14-17. This is a passage used to affirm and confirm the Pentecostal tradition that the purpose of tongues is to provide evidence that one has been validly baptized in the Holy Spirit. Preachers enthusiastically announced that Peter's "this is that" referred to speaking in tongues that accompanied Spirit baptism. Here is a glaring example of eisegesis, that is, reading into a passage what we want it to say rather than extracting what the author actually says. We Pentecostals were desperate to find any scrap of scripture that might support our disputed tradition. I was part of that camp.

It is critically important that we carefully exegete the Joel passage. Of course, Joel says nothing at all about speaking in tongues. His focus is on the universal outpouring of God's Spirit in contrast to the limited outpourings previously experienced. Down through the course of history prior to Pentecost the Holy Spirit had been active. At various times He had anointed different individuals with power and gifts for specific service and ministry. But never had there been an outpouring of the Spirit upon all humanity. Joel had predicted that the time would come when God would usher in the final epoch (last days) of mankind before he established His eternal kingdom. Joel states important characteristics, quoted by Peter in Acts 2:17-18, 21, that mark the beginning of this period and pertain throughout it. Signs that mark the end of this period *"before the coming of the great and glorious day of the Lord"* are indicated in Acts 2:19-20.

What were the divinely given signs which Joel predicted would announce the inauguration of the last age? They are summed up in the first and last statements of Peter's text from Joel. First, instead of a selective outpouring of the Holy Spirit there would now be an outpouring of the Spirit on all humanity. *"In the last days, God says, I will pour out my Spirit on all people"* Acts 2:17a. There would be no gender, age, social, racial, or language barriers that would disqualify anyone from being an equal participant in this universal outpouring. Second, national origin no longer had a bearing upon salvation. It depended upon each individual's response to God. *"Everyone who calls on the name of the Lord will be saved"* Acts 2:21.

The numerous national languages supernaturally displayed at Pentecost were God's dramatic sign that all people groups were now welcome to participate in his kingdom. This was a revolutionary announcement and a total departure from the old Mosaic covenant. This was so revolutionary and such a radical departure from the ancient Jewish tradition that Peter and his fellow disciples totally failed to understand the truth or significance of Joel's prophecy. The sign of "other tongues" signifying the universality of the gospel was obliterated by their adherence to their Jewish tradition. Amazing as it may seem, Peter did not believe the prophetic text from which he preached. He was still emotionally, mentally and spiritually blinded by his biased religious tradition. At this juncture he was sure that only Jews or proselytes (Gentile converts to Judaism) could be saved. It took another series of miracles, dramatically described in Acts 10, before the shackles of his tradition were finally broken.

I have described elsewhere the awesomely painful but freeing process that Peter was subjected to that enabled him to proclaim the gospel to all mankind. The climax of Peter's emancipation was when Jesus sovereignly poured out the Spirit upon the crude, and often despised, soldiers of the Roman army garrison in Caesarea. Without apostolic sanction, without receiving any instruction, without any preconceived ideas of purpose these uncouth Gentiles began to praise God in languages supernaturally uttered. Peter at last understood the purpose of "other tongues". They were the divine sign that no people group was to be called unclean or declared unacceptable into the fellowship of Jesus Christ. Peter finally got the message and made haste to see that these new Spirit anointed believers were baptized in water and welcomed into the infant Church (Acts 10).

Before his Caesarean experienced Peter was like many Pentecostal leaders today. He had been baptized in the Holy Spirit, he was a powerful and successful preacher, he was anointed with multiple gifts of the Spirit including discernment, healing and miracles (Acts 3-5) and yet he was blind to the purpose of tongues. The tentacles of his distorted religious tradition still clung tenaciously to his mind and heart. As a result the Church was crippled and the great commission was in jeopardy. It took a series of divine interventions to free Peter from his obsessive bondage. What will it take to free gifted Pentecostals from their distorted and divisive view of the purpose of tongues? Thank God, there is evidence that change is even now beginning to take place!

five

A FORTHRIGHT STATEMENT

Shortly after my book *Pentecost REVISITED* was published a friend and well known leader in the Assemblies of God asked me this question; "What do you hope to achieve by writing this book?" An honest question deserves a straight answer. My prayer is that my church (for more than 50 years) will dare to seriously reconsider its determined adherence to a tradition that has no solid foundation in Scripture. My hope is that what I have written will be a catalyst toward that end. I am confident that if Scripture is taken seriously we will align with God's Word rather than our divisive tradition. Such a result is not likely unless God intervenes. I know that so I am freed from the stress of trying to do what only God can do. I can write what He has laid on my heart then relax and leave the results with Him.

I am thoroughly Pentecostal, believe in and experience the gifts of the Spirit. Tongues accompanied my own Spirit baptism. I desire genuine supernatural demonstrations of the Holy Spirit to encourage and minister to believers and confound unbelievers. However, I differ strongly with the traditional Pentecostal position that every valid Spirit baptism must be initially evidenced by speaking in tongues, although I once subscribed to this tradition. I point out in *Pentecost REVISITED* (and subsequent articles) that Scripture gives a better and more unifying purpose for tongues and tremendously decreases opportunities for abuse.

A doctrine not founded on biblical truth will produce multiple errors over time. Consider these:

From scripture and personal experience I have seen these errors, abuses and unfortunate results from adhering to our tradition: (1) It deprives the Baptizer, Jesus, to baptize as He wills. There is no Scripture that authorizes limiting the sovereignty of Jesus Christ to baptize as he desires. All He promised regarding Spirit baptism was an endowment of spiritual power and the ability to bear witness to Himself "to the ends of the earth" (Acts 1:8). Many who have never spoken in tongues have experienced both. Should we accept the words of Jesus or our tradition?

(2) This doctrine is a major hindrance to the very unity Christ prayed for, the unity which authenticates Jesus' divine origin (John 17:20-23). (3) Tongues as evidence of Spirit baptism are subject to being counterfeited, manipulated and misused. (4) It can and has led to a spiritual caste system. Christians who haven't spoken in tongues become second class citizens in too many Pentecostal churches. (5) Sincere and persistent seekers who do not receive the "evidence" of tongues become discouraged and even depressed. (6) Some Pentecostal ministers relegate tongues to a mechanical process and actually teach seekers how to manipulate tongue and lips so as to assist the Baptizer provide the necessary "evidence." (7) It can, and sometimes does, elevate the gift above the Giver. (8) It is a doctrine built on assumptions without a solid biblical basis. Surely a doctrine that separates brothers from brothers should have a more substantial foundation. (9) It completely overlooks the critical passage from Joel which Peter quoted at Pentecost in answer to the

question, "What do these tongues mean?" Beyond quoting Joel under the Spirit's inspiration, Peter didn't deal with the question. He was psychologically and spiritually unable to accept the answer Joel articulated.

Joel's prophecy was so monumental and so contrary to Peter's Jewish tradition that he didn't believe the text he quoted. Tongues indicated that the Spirit was now to be poured out on all humanity. Tongues represented every language group, every nation and every race. Peter wasn't ready to accept that and he didn't. It wasn't until he heard the rough Roman soldiers in Caesarea praise God in tongues that he accepted the truth of what the tongues of Pentecost signified. (10) Our tradition ignores the other pertinent Old Testament passage relating to tongues which Paul loosely quotes in First Corinthians 14:21. From this text Paul extracts this principle: "Tongues are a sign, not for believers, but for unbelievers." There is good reason to believe that this applies to generic tongues as outpoured at Pentecost and Caesarea as I explain in my book.(11) A synergistic application of all pertinent scripture leads overwhelmingly to the conclusion that the purpose of tongues accompanying Spirit baptism is to give a sign that all languages, races, nations, and people groups are equally welcome to enter Christ's kingdom. This was a revolutionary concept to the original Jewish Christians who were convinced no one could enter except through the gate of Mosaic legalism.

Pentecostals have blessed the church immeasurably by a renewed emphasis upon the gifts of the Spirit. Supernatural power demonstrated in the operation of some of the gifts has been mightily used to bolster evangelism across Latin America, Asia and Africa. This is true to a lesser degree in USA and

Western Europe. I am convinced most Assemblies of God members are sincere Christians, hungry for God and eager to advance His kingdom. Close friends within the Assemblies of God exemplify integrity and godly character. I love and appreciate them. However, my love for them and my Lord compels me to challenge what scripture convinces me is a flawed creed. It is very troubling to me that most Assemblies of God leaders apparently have closed minds on the issue. Thank God, there are exceptions.

About three year ago I flew to Buffalo, NY where I met with several interested Assemblies of God pastors as well as other ministers. A friend there was responsible for igniting this interest. A veteran and respected Assemblies of God leader in California invited me to meet for dialogue with him. We enjoyed a delightful time of pursuing scriptural truth. I welcome these opportunities and thank God for each one. Why do so many of our leaders discourage open dialogue? I am grateful the Northern California/Nevada District Superintendent encouraged his ministers to engage in dialogue with me. I was disappointed that only one responded. I am still growing in my knowledge of the Lord and his word. I can learn from my brothers if they dared dialogue.

Why the reluctance to research scripture together about the tradition of tongues as required initial evidence of valid Spirit baptism? I can only conjecture so I will. I think some are so emotionally tied to this tradition that it would lead to the melt-down of their egos if they were confronted with scripture that negates their position. There are others who objectively see the lack of biblical support for the accepted tradition but have not discovered a scriptural alternative. That was my situation for many years.

Forty years ago I declared that our tradition was not built on the solid rock of God's word but on the sand of human assumptions. I limited my objection to the annual questionnaire and never publicly proclaimed it. That was my situation for many years until four years ago I was driven to earnestly and prayerfully search the scriptures "to see if these things were so." Insights began to emerge that revealed to me a far more significant purpose for tongues than the divisive tradition that we have adopted.

Others fearfully lament, "If we acknowledge that we missed the Spirit's intent for tongues it will be the death of the Assemblies of God." No, not at all. It will not be the death. It will lead to a glorious resurrection. Of course there can be no resurrection without a prior death. If we do not face this issue head-on and take Spirit-led corrective action, I believe our church will continue in the doldrums. But if we confess we got off track it will make headline news. I believe the curious will flock to Assemblies of God churches, eager to associate with a church body that demonstrates honesty, a spirit of humility and that seeks forgiveness for past error. Jesus will regain His sovereignty to baptize in the Spirit as He wills. Many more believers will be hungry for Jesus to baptize them in the Spirit as He chooses.

Tongues are God's continuing announcement that all language groups, all races, all nations and cultures are equally invited to participate in God's offer of salvation and the Holy Spirit. I believe this is the purpose of tongues that Scripture clearly supports, the character of God demands, and that Jesus' prayer fervently requested.

Many within the ranks of the Assemblies of God have seen the weaknesses connected to our position. I talked to an

Assemblies of God presbyter who agreed with everything in my book but he wasn't willing "to rock the boat." Like many in our secular society, he "went along to get along." I talked to another minister friend recently who has distributed a number of my books. He reported much the same as I have observed. People see the error but don't want to get involved in any corrective action. Where are the Pentecostal men and women who will help generate a demand to have this issue brought before The General Counsel? This was tried in 2009 but discussion of the resolution was squelched. Are there those who will dare make the attempt again?

Naturally, questions have been raised by what I have written. I welcome that. Some of my best insights have resulted from questions I have had to wrestle with. Questions are healthy if they motivate one to search for truth. Here is a question you may have asked yourself, as I certainly have: "If tongues are not the necessary valid physical evidence of Spirit baptism why has there been so much numerical growth among Pentecostals who espouse this position?" I suggest you consider these facts:

A. The Holy Spirit will bless the proclamation of the gospel by whomever it is preached. Paul rejoiced that the gospel was preached even by his enemies who preached out of envy.

B. Misidentifying the purpose of tongues did not nullify the purpose of Spirit baptism (Acts 1:8). I believe scripture affirms the purpose of tongues that accompany Spirit baptism is to signify all races, languages, and people groups are equally welcome into Christ's kingdom, thus promoting unity in the body of Christ. It should not be surprising that Spirit baptism accomplished what the

Spirit ordained be done...anoint believers to proclaim the gospel with power to "the ends of the earth." I firmly believe that if tongues that accompanied Spirit baptisms following Azusa street had been recognized for what they truly were, Christ's sign that all people groups are to be equally welcomed into His body, even greater growth would have resulted. We would have avoided white Pentecostals practicing apartheid in South Africa and flagrant racism in America. Furthermore, abuses, misuses, counterfeit demonstrations and all the disunity and divisiveness associated with making tongues the required initial evidence of Spirit baptism would have been largely avoided.

C. All Pentecostals involved in spectacular growth do not require tongues as proof of Spirit baptism. Renowned *Pentecostal scholar, Dr. Allan Anderson of Birmingham University (England) writes: "Many Pentecostal groups, including some of the largest Pentecostal churches in Europe and Latin America and many in the so-called Charismatic Movement, do not insist on the 'initial evidence' of tongues...It may be very difficult to tell what is meant by 'Pentecostal' today, but perhaps the term is best understood as referring to those movements with an emphasis on the experience of the power of the Holy Spirit with accompanying manifestations of the imminent presence of God." Dr. A. Anderson, "The Origins, growth and significance of the Pentecostal movements of the Third World."* I say a hearty "Amen" to that characterization. It fits the New Testament record and places the emphasis squarely where it should be. I believe adopting these criteria rather than insisting that speaking in tongues is the absolute required evidence of Spirit baptism would produce a plethora of "manifestations of the imminent presence of God."

There is an increasing hunger for genuine supernatural manifestations of the power of God. Frankly, many Christians have seen so much sham, commercialism and fraud associated with elements in Pentecostalism that they have become wary and suspicious about claims of miracles and supernatural manifestations of the Holy Spirit. I believe our tradition has contributed to this sad, sad state of affairs. I am willing to risk suffering, if need be, for the sake of defending truth. There is a sense in which I can even find joy in so doing. I cannot find joy in defending or supporting a questionable and divisive tradition. I now enjoy defending speaking in tongues because I now see the scripturally defined purpose.

When I show people from Scripture that tongues are God's sign that all language groups, races and nationalities are equally precious to God and equally welcome to be part of His kingdom their faces light up. Dialogue does not deteriorate into heated argumentation. I have seen a new openness to supernatural manifestations of the Holy Spirit. Once we Pentecostals get our doctrine concerning the purpose of tongues on a solid biblical foundation much of the abuses that embarrass us will disappear. We will no longer have to cringe when someone begins to relate an embarrassingly unscriptural incident they observed at a Pentecostal service. That will be a great day for biblical Pentecostalism and a great day for advancing God's kingdom with genuine "signs following."

six

THE PURPOSE OF TONGUES THAT
ACCOMPANY SPIRIT BAPTISM

The Pentecostal Movement that broke across Christianity on Azusa Street in Los Angeles in 1906 has impacted every major denomination. It also had a huge impact on my family. My maternal grandparents, Dennis and Laura Bluhm, devout Methodists, were participants in this outpouring of the Holy Spirit not long after Azusa Street. They became Pentecostals about 1912 while living in Kansas. They moved from Kansas to Colorado by covered wagon in 1919 when my mother was 12 years old. Not long after arriving they became involved in establishing an Assemblies of God church in Boulder. My mother, Eunice had surrendered her life to Jesus when she was ten years old. She was filled with the Holy Spirit when she was twelve. Many years later after retiring, Grandpa Bluhm ministered as a lay preacher among the wonderful people living in the Appalachian regions of Virginia and North Carolina.

My dad, Robert Brown, made a commitment to Jesus Christ in 1916 at a Methodist revival held in a country schoolhouse he attended in Danby Valley, Kansas. He was fourteen. His Pentecostal experience of Spirit baptism occurred seven years later when he was twenty-one. Shortly after, he sensed a "call" to full time ministry. In December 1925 my parents were married and soon joined another young couple, the Hoovers, in conducting evangelistic crusades and proclaiming the Pentecostal message across Oklahoma, Arkansas and Kansas. I was born in 1928, the first of eleven children. My earliest memories include going to sleep on hard church benches while mom and dad conducted gospel services. In 1935 my parents moved the family to North Carolina where dad helped "pioneer" an Assemblies of God church. Years later he served as Assistant Superintendent and General Presbyter for the N.C. District Council of the A/G.

I share this family history to underscore that I am a third generation Pentecostal affiliated with the Assemblies of God. (Actually, five generations now). I am very personally concerned with the future of this great fellowship. I have observed and been involved with both the strengths and weaknesses of our movement. I believe our greatest strength is that we bear witness to the fact that the Holy Spirit is again manifesting himself in the Church as he did two thousand years ago. But there are weaknesses in our tradition which need to be corrected if we are to fulfill our destiny. I believe that one significant weakness, indeed, an error, is our strongly held tradition that baptism in the Holy Spirit must always initially be evidenced by speaking in tongues. I address this tradition at length, both historically and theologically, in my books, *Pentecost REVISITED* and *Pentecost REKINDLED.*

Let me first summarize the traditional Pentecostal position. Following that I will present the position I believe Scripture advocates. The traditional position is: "Every valid baptism of believers in the Holy Spirit must be witnessed by the initial physical sign of speaking with other tongues as the Spirit of God gives them utterance (Acts 2:4)". Charles Parham and other early Pentecostals drew the conclusion that since three of the occasions recorded in Acts in which believers were baptized in the Holy Spirit were accompanied by tongues, that must be the evidence of Spirit baptism. It was assumed that the other two occasions where baptism in the Spirit occurs (when Peter and John laid hands on Samaritan believers and Ananias laid hands on Saul of Tarsus) that Spirit baptism was evidenced by tongues. Based on these two assumptions they made the quantum leap to this grand assumption: "every valid Spirit baptism must be physically initially evidenced by speaking in tongues."

At first, my difficulty with our position was three-fold. (1) To build a major doctrine on assumptions provided a faulty foundation. (2) This doctrine brought needless division into the body of Christ. (3) Jesus Christ, the Baptizer, was denied His Sovereignty to baptize as He chose. Further misgivings arose as I observed misuse and abuse of tongues.

I discovered no one seems to have asked the question, "Is there possibly a biblical purpose for tongues other than the traditional Pentecostal position?" If so, where was it located? Surely the Bible would not have left this question unanswered. I determined to search diligently, praying that the Holy Spirit would lead me into truth. I believe my prayer was answered as my eyes were opened to two Old Testament passages that clarify the issues. Why Old Testament? That was the only spiritual "road map" the early disciples had. Therefore, the Holy Spirit illuminated the pertinent Old Testament passages for them... and us. How grateful I was to break out of the fog of traditional ambiguity into the light of scriptural assurance.

Have you ever been lost? I'd guess most people have had experiences of not knowing where they were in relation to where they wanted to be. I've long been amused by the quaint story of the city slicker who took a short cut to his destination across the back-roads of rural Alabama. He became hopelessly disoriented and looked for someone to give him directions. He saw a lad leaning against a fence that bordered the dirt road he was traveling. He stopped, got out of his car and asked the lad, "Boy, can you tell me where I am?" The youngster looked him up and down for a moment, frowning as if in deep thought. Then, as a smile broke across his face, he pointed his finger in the man's direction and announced triumphantly, "There you is!"

I have been lost many times. Once while I was while traveling in East Europe I had hired a van and driver to convey me from Mukachevo, Ukraine to Sigetszenmiklos, Hungary. The driver had no GPS or road map but I assured him I had been to where we were going many times and I would direct him. It so happened the driver entered the town a different way than I was used to. I could spot none of the familiar landmarks I needed to orient myself. How I wished I had a map of the area. Not wanting to admit I was lost I told the driver to keep going through town, hoping I would spot a building or street that would enable me to get my bearings. Eventually I saw a church spire that I knew was near my destination. With the spire as frame of reference I was able to instruct the driver where to go. In a few minutes we were parked in front of the house where I was to spend the night. What a relief.

Sometimes we get lost, or at least confused, on our spiritual journey. Fortunately, we do have a spiritual road map called the Bible that can help us get back on track. I have been studying this "MAP" very diligently in an effort to resolve issues that relate to the baptism in the Holy Spirit when accompanied by tongues as at Pentecost (Acts 2). For a long time I had seen clearly that my church's traditional interpretation of the purpose of such tongues was not solidly based in scripture. It certainly is crystal clear that tongues accompanied Spirit baptism at Pentecost and subsequently at Caesarea and Ephesus. Scripture leaves no doubt about that. But why? What was the purpose of the accompanying tongues?

Put yourself in the Apostle's shoes. He, along with all the other 120 obedient followers of Jesus, had just been baptized in the Holy Spirit as John the Baptist had predicted and as Jesus had promised. Nothing in the Baptist's prediction nor in Jesus's instruction had covered the topic of supernaturally speaking in unknown languages. Peter certainly was no expert on the subject. He was a rank beginner on the subject of pneumatology. After all, the Holy Spirit had been outpoured only minutes before.

There was only one expert present at Pentecost who was thoroughly versed on the activity of the Holy Spirit. He alone knew the meaning and purpose of tongues that accompanied Spirit baptism. Of course, I refer to the Holy Spirit himself. Only He could provide the answer to the question of the curious throng, "What does this mean?" I think Peter realized he was in over his head. I believe he surely must have breathed a silent prayer. "Jesus, you promised that when the Holy Spirit came He would lead us into all truth. He has come and I claim your promise. What shall I tell these thousands of perplexed people? Help me, Holy Spirit!"

Jesus kept his word. The Holy Spirit led Peter to a text from the prophet Joel. Remember, the Old Testament was the authoritative "road map" for the Jews. Peter's text from Joel is the only scripture that defines God's primary purpose for tongues. I have no doubt that Peter's quote was under the immediate and direct inspiration of the Holy Spirit. He said to the inquisitive crowd, *"Fellow Jews and all of you who are in Jerusalem, let me explain this to you; listen carefully to what I say...This is what was spoken by the prophet Joel: 'In the last days, God says, I will pour out my Spirit on all people.'* (Acts 2:14, 16-17a NIV)

As I pondered about the meaning of tongues I realized this is exactly the question the apostle Peter had to deal with following the Spirit's outpouring in Jerusalem. The thousands of Jewish pilgrims who had come from all over the Roman Empire were thoroughly perplexed by the unexpected sound of their native languages being spoken by ignorant Galileans. Peter undoubtedly heard their questions and he knew he must respond. What should he say?

Peter sounds pretty confident as he offers to explain what is happening. This is brash, bold Peter asserting himself. He was good at that. I love his willingness to take risks. The problem is, he promised more than he could deliver. He never does explain the meaning and purpose of tongues. Now here is a surprising truth that is often overlooked. I missed it for many years so if you have noticed this before you are a more alert Bible student than I was. Here's what I overlooked. PETER DIDN'T EXPLAIN HIS TEXT BECAUSE HE DIDN'T BELIEVE IT NOR DID HE PRACTICE IT. Someone may say, "Chaplain, you have gone too far. How can you say Peter didn't believe his text? He preached a great sermon from it and three thousand were saved." But Peter's sermon was from another text that centered on Jesus, the cruci-fied and resurrected Messiah (Christ) whom many in the crowd had rejected fifty days previously. He could preach that sermon with power and authority. However, the meaning and purpose of tongues was a subject he was not yet spiritually capable of dealing with. Acts, chapter ten, makes this exceedingly clear.

Understanding the prophecies of Old Testament prophets Joel and Isaiah clearly reveal the purposes of tongues outpoured at Pentecost and subsequently.

Let's do what Peter failed to do. Follow along as we explain the text from Joel. You will notice that Joel says nothing at all about tongues although they had caused the question. His focus is on the universal outpouring of the Holy Spirit which is to characterize the "last days". This is in sharp contrast to the very limited outpouring in previous ages. Down through the course of history prior to Pentecost the Spirit of God had been active. At various times he had anointed different individuals with gifts for specific service and ministry, mostly prophets within Israel. But never had there been an outpouring of the Spirit upon all humanity. At last, the fulfillment of Joel's prophecy was at hand. What the inspired prophet had predicted must usher in the final age (last days) was happening in Jerusalem. Thousands watched and listened in wonder and bewilderment.

What were the signs which Joel predicted would announce the inauguration of the "last days"? They are summed up in the first and last statements from Joel's prophecy. First, instead of a selective outpouring of the Spirit upon a few there would now be an outpouring upon all humanity. There would be no gender barriers, no age barriers, no social, racial or language barriers that would disqualify a person from being eligible to receive the Holy Spirit. (Acts 2:17) Second, national origin no longer had a bearing upon salvation. It depended upon each individual's response to the gospel. *"Everyone who calls on the name of the Lord will be saved."* (Acts 2:21)

The numerous national languages supernaturally displayed at Pentecost were God's dramatic sign that all language groups were now equally welcome to be part of His kingdom. From our perspective we can scarcely imagine how revolutionary this concept was to Peter and the other disciples. They completely failed to grasp what Joel said. The sign of "other tongues" pointing to the universality of the gospel was obliterated by bondage to their now outmoded tradition. Peter couldn't explain Joel's prophecy because he didn't believe it. He was still emotionally, mentally and spiritually blinded by his biased religious tradition. At this time in his life, despite spending three years under the tutelage of Jesus, he was still convinced that only Jews or proselytes (Gentile converts to Judaism) could be saved. It took a series of miracles, dramatically described in Acts 10, before the shackles of his tradition were finally broken.

The climax of Peter's emancipation is vividly described in Acts 10. It began in Joppa and culminated in Caesarea. When Jesus sovereignly poured out His Spirit upon the crude, despised soldiers of the Roman occupation army stationed in Caesarea, Peter's fetters were loosened. Without apostolic sanction, without any previous instruction, without any preconceived ideas relating to baptism in the Holy Spirit, these uncouth Gentiles began to praise God in languages supernaturally uttered. The tongues were not a sign to the Gentiles but to Peter and his Jewish friends. Bound by their tradition, they did not believe Gentiles were eligible to receive the Holy Spirit or be part of God's kingdom. Caesarea proved them wrong.

Peter at last understood the purpose of what had happened at Pentecost. The significance of Joel's prophecy, the relevance of the house top visions in Joppa and now the surprising outpouring of the Spirit in Caesarea upon Gentiles convinced Peter of the true purpose of tongues. They were the divine sign that no language group, no race and no nationality was to be called unclean or unacceptable into the fellowship of Jesus Christ. Having at last got the message, Peter ordered that these new Spirit anointed believers be baptized in water and welcomed into the infant church.

Before his experience in Caesarea Peter was like many Pentecostal leaders today. He had been baptized in the Holy Spirit, he was a powerful and successful preacher, he was anointed with multiple gifts of the Spirit including discernment, healing, tongues and miracles (Acts 2-5). Nevertheless, he was absolutely blind to the purpose of tongues which his Joel text at Pentecost clearly revealed. The tentacles of his outmoded and biased religious tradition still clung tenaciously to his mind and heart. As a result, the church was crippled and the great commission was in jeopardy. It took a series of divine interventions to free Peter from his obsessive bondage. What will it take to free gifted Pentecostals from their distorted and divisive tradition concerning the purpose of tongues. Only God knows but I believe it must and will happen.

The second pertinent passage which includes an Old Testament quotation is in I Corinthians 14:20-22. Here is the apostle Paul's loose quotation from Isaiah 28:11-12; *"In the law it is written: 'Through men of strange tongues and through the lips of foreigners I will speak to this people, but even then they will not listen to me,' says the Lord."* From this Isaiah passage Paul extracts a key principle; *"TONGUES, THEN, ARE A SIGN, NOT FOR BELIEVERS, BUT FOR UNBELIEVERS."* (I Corinthians 14:22a)

First, consider the Old Testament passage upon which Paul bases this principle. We know Paul used examples from the Old Testament era to serve as lessons for the Christian era. For example, Paul employs Hagar and Sarah as symbols of two covenants. Hagar, mother of Ishmael by Abraham, represented the Old Covenant of law. Sarah, mother of Isaac, represented the New Covenant of grace (Galatians 4:21-31). It seems that Paul is making a similar parallelism between "strange tongues" of the Old Testament quotation and "tongues" in the Christian era (I Corinthians 14:21-22a). Paul may very well be using "tongues" in a generic sense. If so, I Corinthians 14:22a must include all instances where tongues are publicly spoken en masse in an approved fashion. How do I come to that conclusion? Simply by applying what Paul says in verse 23. Here Paul declares the unbelievers who observe a congregation all speaking in tongues en masse would conclude they are crazy.

The context makes it plain that the apostle discouraged such behavior in the strongest terms. This sort of display was not a sign for unbelievers. Verse 22a can't apply here to this disapproved display of en masse tongues. Nor does it apply to praying in tongues since this is private, between an individual and God. Nor does it apply to a message in tongues with interpretation since this is equivalent to prophecy. Furthermore, the "then" of verse 22 obviously refers to the Old Testament example in verse 21. In the Old Testament example, tongues are clearly spoken en masse "through men of strange tongues," i.e., the Assyrian captors. Who are these "strange tongues" addressing? They are speaking to the chosen people of the Old Covenant who are being carried into Assyrian captivity because of unbelief and disobedience.

We have established that verse 22a doesn't apply to tongues in the Corinthian church. To try to apply it there leads to confusion and insurmountable difficulty. Where in the New Testament record are tongues spoken en masse with apostolic approval? Why, of course, when Jesus baptized groups of believers in the Holy Spirit. This first happened in Jerusalem to the one hundred-twenty at Pentecost. This outpouring of the Spirit is unique. It ushers in the new Christian era of grace and ushers out the old Mosaic era of law. Or as Paul might say, Hagar was expelled and Sarah was installed.

John the Baptist was the last Old Testament prophet and he prepared the way for Jesus, the Author of the New Covenant. Because this was a tremendously significant and unique occasion our Lord Jesus provided a very special sign to accompany the initial outpouring of the Holy Spirit. He anointed his disciples to speak in languages unknown to them but clearly understood by the thousands of assembled Jewish pilgrims. This is the only New Testament record of tongues not understood by the speakers being understood by others without an interpreter.

These tongues were not a sign or evidence to the one hundred-twenty that they had been baptized in the Holy Spirit. How can I be sure of that? First, consider this: John the Baptist had predicted Jesus would baptize "with the Holy Spirit and with fire." The disciples saw the fire dancing over each head when the Spirit fell upon them. This was the evidence that certified Jesus had kept his promise. Indeed, the Comforter had come just as Jesus had promised. Neither John nor Jesus had ever said anything about tongues so they had no meaning or purpose as far as the one hundred-twenty were concerned. Please follow along closely because this is pivotal. The "unbelievers" for whom the tongues are a sign are the thousands of Jews who have gathered in Jerusalem to celebrate the feast of Pentecost. What was it they didn't believe? They didn't believe that Jesus, the crucified rabbi from Nazareth, was really their Messiah. Now, Paul's declaration that tongues are a sign to unbelievers makes all the sense in the world.

In the parallelism of Paul, these pilgrims compare to the chosen people of the Old Testament who are in captivity because they didn't believe or obey Jehovah. Neither had these religious tourists believed the Old Testament prophets who pointed them to a suffering Messiah. Some of them had actually participated in the crucifixion of their Messiah (Acts 2:23). As these unbelievers heard the divinely appointed "sign" of tongues they were startled out of their complacency and began to ask serious questions. Perplexed, they enquired, "How can these unlettered Galileans declare 'the wonders of God' in our native languages.? What is the meaning of all this?" You can be sure Peter had their full attention when he arose to respond to the enquiries. The "sign" to these unbelievers had fulfilled its purpose. We will have more to say about the results of Peter's sermon a little later.

We have carefully considered the Corinthian text. Now let's review the facts upon which most if not all can agree. (1) In the Old Testament context the "strange tongues" are the languages spoken by the Assyrian conquerors of the Jews. (2) "This people" refers to the Jews, God's chosen people, in captivity. (3) It is God's chosen people (although disobedient) who are the unbelievers who will not listen to the truth God is conveying through judgment. (4) In Paul's illustration, the "strange tongues" from the Old Testament quotation parallels the "tongues" in verse 22a. (5) The "then" of I Corinthians 14:22a bridges the gap between what happened in the Old Testament and what is happening in the New Testament era. I think there is wide agreement so far.

The point that Paul makes from the Old Testament and the application he makes for the New Testament era is this: *"TONGUES, THEN, ARE A SIGN, NOT FOR BELIEVERS BUT FOR UNBELIEVERS."* It is this application that creates confusion and where unanimity ends. The only thing most agree on is that the text in its immediate context doesn't make sense. J.B. Phillips, the Bible translator, has this notation on the bottom of the page referencing this verse: "*This is the sole instance of the translator's departing from the accepted text. He felt bound to conclude, from the sense of the next three verses, that we have here either a slip of the pen on Paul's part, or, more probably, a copyist's error." (p. 373 THE NEW TESTAMENT IN MODERN ENGLISH.)

I strongly suggest this is not a slip of Paul's pen nor a copyist's error. The apostle meant exactly what is recorded. Of course, it doesn't make sense in the immediate context because Paul is laying down a principle that applies universally to a much wider context. Let's review some points already alluded to (1) Tongues spoken en masse when Christians congregate would appear a sign of insanity to unbelievers present (I Corinthians 14:23). (2) Paul uses an Old Testament text as the basis for the principle he lays down in verse 22a. This would indicate that the principle is generic and not applicable just in Corinth. This seems obvious since otherwise approved tongues would either be private communication with God (prayer in the Spirit) or regulated tongues with interpretation, equivalent to prophecy. I Corinthians 14:22a would not apply in either case. (3) Are there other instances in the New Testament where tongues are spoken en masse in addition to the Corinthian passage? Yes, in

Jerusalem at Pentecost, in Caesarea, in Ephesus and perhaps in Samaria when Jesus baptized believers in the Holy Spirit. In these instances the en masse speaking in tongues is obviously approved and not forbidden. We have already considered the Day of Pentecost episode in Jerusalem. Let's now observe what happened to the recipients of the Spirit in Samaria and Caesarea. (I look at Ephesus and Saul in my book *Pentecost REVISITED*.)

Could it be that Paul's general principle drawn from the Old Testament applies to these occasions of Spirit baptism? Absolutely. I can see no reason why not. If this principle, *"Tongues, then,* ('then' refers back to the OT text) *are a sign, not for believers but for unbelievers"* has relevance to the other en masse speaking in tongues then Paul's assertion makes sense. (The "other en masse speaking in tongues", of course, occurred when Jesus baptized the European Gentiles in Caesarea and the Asian Gentiles in Ephesus in the Holy Spirit and perhaps the Samaritans.) But this leads to other questions, "Who are the unbelievers in each instance and what is it they do not believe? Could the "unbelievers" Paul refers to possibly be God's chosen people in the New Testament era, i.e., followers of Jesus?" It would certainly continue to maintain the parallelisms between the two passages. And even at the unique outpouring on Pentecost, which marked the end of the Old Testament era and the beginning of the Church age, all the Spirit filled disciples were "unbelievers" in the sense they did not believe Gentiles could be part of the Messianic kingdom without submitting to Jewish rites. But in this transition period the Jewish pilgrims could be considered still under the old covenant.

Let's look briefly at the broader context relating to the work of the Holy Spirit. Extensive teaching relating to the work of the Spirit is given by Jesus in John's gospel, chapters 14 through 17.

The fervent longing of Jesus is contained in his prayer in chapter 17. Listen to his heart cry. "My prayer is not for them (disciples) alone. I pray also for those who will believe in me through their message, that all of them may be one, just as you are in me and I am in you. May they also be in us so that the world may believe that you have sent me." John 17:20-21. It was the Holy Spirit's task to help believers achieve this unity that Christ prayed for.

Now let's apply this truth to what took place on the day of Pentecost. After the curiosity of the unbelievers had been aroused by the sign of tongues, they were eager to hear Peter's explanation of what it all meant. Of course, he couldn't explain Joel because he didn't believe the truth Joel proclaimed. The truth, according to Joel, was that the supernaturally spoken languages symbolized that all the languages of the world had access to the gospel without submitting to Jewish rites. This was anathema to Peter and the other disciples. He immediately changed texts and preached a powerful sermon that the Holy Spirit used to bring three thousand new converts into the church.

Three thousand new believers at Pentecost gave evidence of being filled with the Holy Spirit. It wasn't tongues but something far more significant and compelling...loving unity.

We can't forget that these new Christians were from at least fifteen different countries. Each country had its own language and culture, and likely, each citizen thought that his own was superior to the others. But when they responded in faith to Peter's summons to repentance and baptism a remarkable transformation took place. "All the believers were together and had everything in common. Selling their possessions and goods, they gave to anyone as he had need." (Acts 2:44-45) Who was it that sold their possessions? It must have been the Jews who lived in Judea. And who was it who had needs with whom the local Christians gladly shared their possessions? Why of course, those wandering pilgrims from Parthia, Media, Egypt, Phrygia and the other distant lands.

Despite their nationalistic pride and cultural differences they became united in Christ. The Holy Spirit immediately began the work of bringing Christ's prayer for unity to fruition. (After Azusa, why didn't we assign this unity, that response in love to new brothers and sisters in Christ, as a sign of Spirit baptism? Could it be because cultural racism was so entrenched that our early leaders didn't dare consider uniting with our black brothers? I don't know the answer but I do know something of the power of tradition, both cultural and religious.)

Now let's continue our investigation of Spirit baptisms and en masse speaking in tongues. The next recorded instance of believers being baptized in the Holy Spirit is found in Acts 8:14-17. Philip the evangelist conducted a highly successful evangelistic campaign in one of the Samaritan cities. Many turned to Christ and were baptized in water. The word got back to Jerusalem and the apostolic leadership sent Peter and John to find out what was going on in Samaria. They immediately discovered the new Christians had not yet been baptized in the Holy Spirit. I'm sure this must have created a question in the minds of Peter and John. Why the delay in outpouring the Spirit upon these new believers. Were these half-breed Samaritans really eligible to be included in the company of Christ's followers? There was one test that could resoundingly affirm that they were. As Peter and John prayed over them and placed their hands upon them, they received the Holy Spirit.

Pentecostal tradition assumes they spoke in tongues at this time. Certainly something unusual took place otherwise the magician would not have tried to purchase the ability to make it happen. If speaking in tongues did accompany the Samaritan's baptism in the Holy Spirit, as I assume it did, what was the purpose? Exactly what Paul said, a sign to unbelievers. Who were the unbelievers? Certainly Peter and John and perhaps other Jewish Christians who may have been present. We know Peter and John were racists. Only weeks before John had wanted to incinerate a Samaritan village that had been inhospitable to Jesus and the disciples. (Luke 9:54) And we know Peter prided himself on not associating with anyone "unclean." The Samaritans were of mixed pagan and Jewish blood and were despised by the Jews. But the outpouring of the Spirit upon the Samaritan converts trumped the prejudices of Peter and John. Jesus' prayer for unity was being answered. Another "unacceptable" people group had been added to the broadening circle of Christians.

Acts 10 provides a tremendously dramatic account of Jesus invading the Gentile world. Peter was drafted as a reluctant chaplain to go share the gospel with the Roman garrison in Caesarea. Peter was definitely out of his comfort zone. For moral support he took several Jewish Christians with him. Arriving in Caesarea, Peter greeted Cornelius briefly and then quickly began to present the gospel. Shortly after Peter began his sermon, Jesus, the Baptizer, interrupted him and poured out the Holy Spirit upon the assembled household and soldiers of Cornelius. There is no doubt that these "unclean" Gentiles began to speak in tongues when the Spirit was outpoured. Peter and his Jewish companions were utterly flabbergasted. How could this be? It was contrary to every facet of their Jewish tradition. But their tradition was not in control. Jesus, the Baptizer, was in charge and he had ushered these Gentiles into His family and poured out his Spirit upon them.

Peter recognized the authority of his sovereign Lord by immediately declaring that the Gentile converts should be baptized in water. Without any teaching about the Holy Spirit, with no knowledge of tongues, without seeking any experience, Jesus simply, in divine sovereignty, filled these Gentiles with His Spirit. So what was the purpose of tongues. Obviously, it was to convince the tradition bound Jews that the Gentiles were welcome into the household of Jesus Christ. They had not believed that possible. But, as the apostle Paul said, tongues were meant to be a sign to the unbelievers. Tongues certainly were the sign that convinced Peter and other Jewish Christians who didn't believe pagan Gentiles could be welcomed into the church without first undergoing Jewish rites. A replication of the tongues of Pentecost shattered their disbelief.

The tradition that Gentiles could only enter the church by submitting to Jewish ordinances was firmly entrenched in the minds of all Jewish Christians. Word got back to the church in Jerusalem that Peter had been fraternizing with uncircumcised Gentiles. He was roundly criticized for his indiscretion. Peter could understand their frustration since he would have been one of their number a few weeks previously. He patiently explained the whole situation, concluding with this clincher: *"Just as I was starting to speak, the Holy Spirit came on them as he had come on us at the beginning. Then I remembered what the Lord had said, 'John baptized with water, but you will be baptized with the Holy Spirit.' So if God gave them the same gift as he gave us when we believed in the Lord Jesus Christ, who was I to think that I could oppose God."* How could it be presented more clearly that the tongues of Pentecost repeated to the Gentiles were a sign to the tradition-bound Jews that Jesus himself had accepted these uncircumcised foreigners? Babel was being reversed. Jesus' prayer for unity among all His followers was being realized in an expanding circle of people groups.

We can safely assert that the Holy Spirit never does anything that hinders the prayer of Jesus from being realized (John 17). And yet the traditional Pentecostal interpretation of tongues that accompany Spirit baptism has been extremely divisive within the larger body of Christ. Let me emphasize that tongues themselves have not produced disunity. Rather, the insistence that tongues must validate every Spirit baptism has created division. It logically follows that if tongues are to help rather than to hinder the fulfillment of Jesus' prayer for unity amongst His followers there must be another reason why tongues accompany baptism in the Holy Spirit. I have pointed out how the application of the apostle Paul's declaration (I Corinthians 14:22) to the various outpourings of the Spirit in Acts clearly reveals that the accompanying tongues were for the sake of those who didn't believe. What didn't they believe? They didn't believe that every people group should be welcomed into Christian fellowship without first undergoing Jewish rites.

But that was in the New Testament era at the beginning of the outpouring of the Holy Spirit. How about today? Does speaking in tongues still accompany Spirit baptism? Without doubt it does but not always and not of necessity. Jesus, the sovereign Baptizer, determines how he chooses to express Himself in the baptism experience. (See the Epilogue in *Pentecost REVISITED*) And the purpose of tongues is not to authenticate Spirit baptism. It remains essentially the same today as it was in the book of Acts. The purpose is to be a sign that no people group is to be excluded from Christ's kingdom.

Tongues are an ongoing reminder that we are to except one another as equals in the body of Christ. Paul exhorts the Ephesian church: *"Make every effort to keep the unity of the Spirit through the bond of peace. There is one body and one Spirit..."* (Eph. 4:3-4a) This understanding is important universally but especially so in Africa and parts of Asia and South America where tribal divisions produce deadly conflict. As our American society becomes more diverse it will become increasingly pertinent for us. Whenever the Holy Spirit provides a spiritual language it is to remind us that no spiritual gift is of value unless motivated by LOVE which produces unity. (I Cor. 13.)

We make tongues a sign or an evidence that believers have been filled with the Spirit despite no solid biblical basis. But our tradition goes beyond that and concludes that if believers do not speak in tongues they are not filled with the Spirit. It is this conclusion that is divisive and has not one scriptural text to support it. I have seen the abuse that has resulted from this conclusion. Despite genuine efforts to prevent abuse there is an insidious temptation to bow to denominational pressure to speak in tongues. This has led to manipulations and counterfeit expressions. We must make a huge assumption to conclude that the tongues of Pentecost were meant to be evidence to the disciples that they had been baptized in the Holy Spirit. This had never been mentioned in John's prophecy or in Jesus' teaching. But in view of the apostle's clear declaration that tongues are intended to be a sign to unbelievers, not to believers, our tradition becomes clearly untenable if Scripture is to be our guide.

Two pertinent, extended contexts that deal with the ministry of the Holy Spirit are John 14-17 and I Corinthians 12-14. In John 14 and 16, Jesus emphasizes the teaching ministry of the Holy Spirit. In chapter fifteen Jesus speaks of the fruit of the Spirit that grows out of a close connection with himself. In John 17 he concludes with His loving, tender prayer for unity amongst His followers. The Holy Spirit is His agent to help produce the unity for which He prayed.

In the Corinthian passage (Ch. 12) Paul gives instruction concerning manifestation of the diverse spiritual gifts which the Lord has given to the Church. Despite the diversity of gifts, it is the Spirit's goal to bridge all social, racial, economic and cultural differences. He will not have accomplished his purpose until all followers of Jesus Christ are brought into harmonious spiritual unity. He graphically describes the unifying purpose of baptism by the Spirit in I Corinthians 12:12-13. Chapter thirteen is Paul's marvelous ode to love. Here he emphasizes the uselessness and vanity of spiritual gifts if they are not ministered in love and humility. In chapter 14 he explains the purpose of the vocal gifts and how and when they are to be exercised, particularly tongues and prophecy. The edification or building up of the church is the purpose of these gifts. Therefore, the gift of tongues is not to be used in the church except in conjunction with the gift of interpretation. En masse speaking in tongues by a church congregation is not permitted. This sort of manifestation leads to confusion, does not edify, and unbelieving observers would conclude the speakers are crazy.

When we consider these teachings by Jesus and Paul, something significant stands out. The culmination of the Spirit's teaching ministry, his empowering ministry and his gifting ministry is to produce followers of Jesus that are in unity with one another and with their common Lord across every barrier that divides people. Any interpretation of the Spirit's ministry that does not advance this goal is an incorrect interpretation.

It should be discarded and replaced by an interpretation that furthers the goal of the Spirit.

My church's interpretation of tongues that accompany Spirit baptism leads to disunity within the body of Christ and sometimes results in a spiritual caste system within the church itself. Since there is another interpretation that is supported by the overall context of scripture as well as by specific texts, why reject it? Is the glue of tradition more binding than Scripture?

There is one other issue I must address that makes it difficult for the Assemblies of God to break the shackles of their tradition. Many Assemblies of God adherents, like me, experienced speaking in tongues when initially filled with the Holy Spirit. As a result of my experience I assumed that our tradition was correct, that is, every valid Spirit baptism must be authenticated by speaking in tongues. What led me to challenge this teaching? (Let me insert here that I never have challenged the reality of my experience or the value of speaking in tongues.)

Several factors led to my change of mind and heart. First, I had a hunger for truth and I was determined to follow revealed truth wherever it would lead. Second, I came into contact with godly men who had never sought tongues but clearly demonstrated powerful gifts and graces imparted by the Spirit. Third, I came to know men who confessed to me that they had sought the gift of tongues to accompany Spirit baptism. Despite their earnest seeking and willingness to speak as the Spirit gave utterance, their prayers regarding tongues went unanswered. They were not enabled to speak in tongues but Jesus assures us they received the Holy Spirit (Luke 11:13). These same men today are being significantly used to advance God's kingdom.

These realities led to a search for scripture that would give a solid theological and biblical basis for our tradition. The best I could come up with for our own claim was a chain of assumptions. It was assumed that all baptisms in the Holy Spirit recorded in Acts were accompanied by tongues. That is not an illogical assumption and could well be true. This led to another assumption that became our imbedded tradition, namely, EVERY VALID SPIRIT BAPTISM MUST BE ACCOMPANIED BY THE INITIAL PHYSICAL EVIDENCE OF SPEAKING IN TONGUES. I am convinced this conclusion is illogical and unscriptural. Our early leaders apparently never asked the question, "Could there possibly be some other reason why tongues accompanied the outpouring of the Holy Spirit?"

When I realized that our "distinctive" tradition was built upon assumptions and not a clear declaration of Scripture I began searching for a more biblical reason for Spirit inspired tongues. It was then I saw the significance of Isaiah as quoted in First Corinthians 14:21-22a. Using Paul's explanation for legitimate tongues when multiple believers are speaking at the same time, I was forced to consider the Spirit baptisms in Acts. Knowing that I must consider the whole context of scripture for a proper understanding of tongues I began to identify pertinent passages. One such passage is Acts 1:8. Here Jesus announces the Holy Spirit will provide power for his followers to be effective witnesses to their Lord throughout the worldwide community. What were the impediments to this universal witness that must be combated? Nationalism, religious and cultural elitism and racial prejudices were powerful barriers that would prevent the gospel from penetrating "the ends of the earth."

For a striking illustration of racism inherent in ancient Judaism consider what happened when Jesus preached his first sermon in his home town of Nazareth.

If you doubt the pervasive influence of religious elitism and prejudice within Judaism in the New Testament era please read carefully Luke 4:14-29. I invite you to consider these important truths revealed in this passage: (1) Jesus began his public preaching ministry in the synagogue of Nazareth, his home town, under the powerful anointing of the Holy Spirit [vss 14, 18]. (2) The congregation initially applauded his teaching [vs. 22]. (3) Directed by the Holy Spirit, Jesus presents the truth introduced in the Old Testament that God's loving concern for people is universal, extending even to people the Jews considered their enemies [vss 26-27]. (4) Jesus' message triggered a murderous rage within the hearts of his own townsmen and they attempted to violently silence his voice [vss 28-29]. (5) There are multiple examples that this attitude permeated Judaism at this time. (Consider James' and John's desire to incinerate the Samaritans and the intense persecution of Paul, the apostle to the Gentiles). How was the Holy Spirit going to transform the thinking of those first Jewish followers from rabid racists into visionary ambassadors for his universal, eternal Kingdom?

Could it be possible that Jesus designated tongues to accompany Spirit baptism in order to combat these powerful elitist attitudes? Indeed, I believe he did. The symbolism was powerful for the Jews. God had produced a profusion of "other tongues" at Babel which resulted in confusion and separation. At Pentecost, God provided "other tongues" as a means of overcoming the effects of Babel. It is apparent in John 14-17 and I Corinthians 12-14 that Jesus' grand goal was to create a new order of human beings united in loyalty and love to Him and to one another. It was the task of the Holy Spirit to provide power and incentive to make this unbelieving, who just happened to be Jewish Christians. The purpose of tongues is clearly to promote unity within the universal body of Christ. No people group is to be excluded. That continues to be the purpose of tongues that accompanies Spirit baptism, our tradition to the contrary. As we continue to insist on our traditional interpretation are we in danger of falling into the subtle trap of religious elitism? Indeed, many Pentecostal churches have already fallen into that trap.

In addition to the lack of sound biblical support, I found an historical basis for questioning the legitimacy of our tradition. Charles Parham was the religious leader that, according to Assemblies of God historian Edith Blumhofer, introduced the "association between tongues and the baptism of the Holy Spirit." She goes on to say, "And it was that association that gave identity to the scattered fledgling restorationist, millenarian constituency that became American Pentecostalism." (The A/G, Vol I, p. 92) What do we know about Charles Parham, the father of our disputed tradition? Again I quote Blumhofer, "Despite Parham's denials, his worldview nurtured racist assumptions, which frequently surfaced.... As the Movement attracted some who were concerned to balance spiritual experience with doctrinal orthodoxy, he responded by emphasizing his private interpretations of Scripture. He proved unwilling to work graciously with a black man, writing cuttingly of Seymour's Los Angeles mission..." (Ibid, p. 89, 91)

I found Blumhofer's description of Parham's doctrinal inventiveness very revealing. It "led to his advocating a variety of unusual interpretations of Scripture to meet such age-old questions as 'Where did Cain get his wife?' For example, he distinguished between 'created' and 'formed' humanity, claiming that all 'created' humanity perished in the flood, whereas, through Noah, Adam's line of 'formed' humanity was preserved. Thus, Cain's wife was created, whereas Cain was formed. Parham also subscribed to Anglo-Israelism, a view that maintained that the Anglo-Saxon peoples were the ten lost tribes of Israel...The sense of Anglo-Saxon superiority nourished by his eschatology corresponded neatly with racial attitudes that pervaded much of the turn-of-the-century Protestant culture." (Ibid, p.75-76). This historical background gave me a better understanding of why Parham overlooked the real purpose of tongues accompanying Spirit baptism. It would have necessitated him to accept his black brethren on an equal footing. This is not to say that Parham had no redeeming qualities. He did and God used him despite his imperfections. But he was a child of his traditional culture and tradition won out over scriptural principles.

There is another aspect of Spirit baptism accompanied by tongues plainly revealed in Scripture but largely ignored by us Pentecostals. In keeping with our American tradition of individualism, we emphasize individuals receiving the baptism in the Holy Spirit. Not so in Scripture where the Holy Spirit was almost universally poured out upon people groups and families. The purpose was to affirm these groups and families were united in fellowship by the Spirit with the new Kingdom of God (Church) born at Pentecost. What would happen if, being Kingdom oriented rather than individually oriented, we prayed for people groups and extended families to be filled with the Spirit?

Our traditional doctrine keeps us focused on the individual's experience of speaking in tongues. Of course individuals are important. Jesus dealt with me as an individual and my Spirit baptism was accompanied by speaking in tongues. When this happened I sensed I had a special bond, almost a mystical, spiritual unity with those first filled at Pentecost 1900 years previously. Only later did I see that this was exactly what scripture indicated tongues were supposed to do.

Tongues often do accompany Spirit baptism and can be a sign or evidence of Spirit activity but not THE exclusive sign or evidence of Spirit baptism. In the early church, and today, their primary purpose is to promote unity among diverse people groups and to relate them back to the apostles at Pentecost. Could this be true "apostolic succession" rather than that advocated by Rome? In the face of militant, materialistic atheism, religious humanism and violent, fundamentalist Islam the power of the Holy Spirit, demonstrated through a loving, united Church, is increasingly essential.

For forty years I have protested the manner in which my church has put our Lord in a box. When we deprive the Baptizer of his sovereign power to choose how, where and when he will baptize, we have overstepped our authority in an arrogant way. If non-Christians are present when Jesus chooses to have tongues accompany en masse Spirit baptisms, the awesome presence of God will be so pervasive that unbelievers will acknowledge something supernatural has occurred. Tongues will indeed be a sign to them. If we insist tongues must validate every Spirit baptism we rob Jesus of his sovereignty. As a result of clinging to our tradition a variety of unnecessary abuses have arisen which our critics have been quick to publicize. I have sadly acknowledged some of them in my book *Pentecost REVISITED*. I long for, I ache for, the reality of the divine Presence so powerfully mediated that there will be no place for sham and counterfeit.

Tongues are without profit unless they help produce the loving unity for which they were divinely ordained. I believe tongues, when they accompany Spirit baptism, are Jesus' way of reminding us that the Holy Spirit is reversing the curse of Babel. The tongues of Babel produced clamor and division. The tongues of Pentecost were designed to promote unity. Once we see tongues in this light we will be motivated to build bridges that bring believers together rather than erect walls that separate. If the Assemblies of God and associated churches take the lead in affirming the unifying purpose of speaking in tongues, new life will erupt throughout our Pentecostal fellowship; barriers will come down, churches will grow and our Lord will be glorified.

seven

A WORK IN PROGRESS

Pentecost REVISITED is a work in progress. I deal with multiple issues that confront the church of Jesus Christ. As a long-time member of the Assemblies of God I relate my journey that led me to reject a central tenet of my denomination. From its beginning in 1914 the Assemblies of God had insisted there could be no valid baptism in the Holy Spirit unless it was initially accompanied by speaking in tongues. My parents were devout members of the Assemblies of God; my dad a minister and District official for many years. I was thoroughly indoctrinated in the Assemblies of God tradition of Spirit baptism and tongues.

A legalistic approach to "holiness" was prevalent in many churches when I was growing up in the 1930's and 1940's. My dad came under the influence of legalism to the extent that he disapproved of my participating in school sports. Such activities were too "worldly." I loved sports, particularly football and basketball, and insisted on playing. Mother became a moderating influence on dad and I was permitted to play. However, he never attended any of my games although I was the star player of the small high school where I played basketball. As a result I equated Christianity with legalism and rejected the baby with the bath water. I had plans for my life that centered around athletics, not as a player but as a coach. I didn't want to serve a God who disapproved of something that I wanted to pursue as a life career.

As a consequence of my distorted view of Christianity I rebelled against the very idea of becoming a Christian and chose to go my own way and do my own thing. After graduating from high school in 1946 I joined the U.S. Army Air Corps (predecessor of the U.S. Air Force) later that year. My motive was to gain the benefits of the G.I. Bill for college. Fortunately, I discovered going my own way and doing my own thing was not all I thought it would be. While stationed at Randolph Field near San Antonio, Texas in 1947-48 Uncle Sam allowed me to attend Trinity University in the evening. One of my classes influenced me to think more deeply about life and my future.

I had become an amateur agnostic. I hoped there was no God because I didn't want to have to answer to Him for my life. But some of my studies at the University compelled me to ask; "What if God does exist? What if God really did come among us in the person of Jesus Christ? What if the Bible paints a realistic picture of humanity? What if God loves me and has a purpose for my life that begins in time but continues for eternity? How could I know for sure the answers to my questions?"

I share the story of how God got through to me and my subsequent spiritual pilgrimage in *Pentecost REVISITED*. I also describe being baptized in the Holy Spirit and my experience of speaking in tongues which accompanied my baptism. As a consequence of committing my life and will to Jesus Christ I underwent a major career change. Instead of coaching athletes He called me to become a spiritual coach in the great game of life. I became a pastor and a career chaplain in the U.S. Navy where I served mostly with the U.S. Marines.

After graduating from Denver Seminary in 1958 I was ordained by the Rocky Mountain District of the Assemblies of God. Less than two years later I was called to active duty from a pastorate in Granby, Colorado to serve as a chaplain in the Navy. I loved the opportunity the Navy gave me to minister to young men and women across denominational lines.

I appreciated my church and was thoroughly Pentecostal as far as valuing the gifts of the Spirit operating in the church. However, my search of scripture led me to clearly see that our tradition concerning tongues was built on a series of assumptions with no solid scriptural basis. When I was in Vietnam in 1968-69 the Lord very clearly let me know I had to honestly confess my variance to my denomination. I determined to do so when I returned from Vietnam even though it might result in my removal from the chaplaincy. How God protected me despite some leaders who called for my dismissal is a major thread running through the book. God had some wonderful men in key leadership roles who valued my ministry despite my rejection of our tradition.

What convinces me that the Assemblies of God position on tongues is not supported by scripture or reason? Consider these issues. (1) This doctrinal tradition produces disunity in the body of Christ. I studied Jesus' teaching on the Holy Spirit in John 14, 15 and 16 followed by His prayer for unity among His followers "so that the world may believe that you have sent me." John. 17:21b. The Holy Spirit is the Divine Agent for bringing believers into unity. It did not seem reasonable or even possible for Jesus to ordain something that would oppose what he prayed for. I believe this can be accepted as a Christian axiom: "Any teaching that promotes unity among Christians believers is of God. Any teaching that promotes division and separation among believers is of human origin."

(2) This tradition put God in a box he didn't create. It robbed Jesus of His sovereignty to baptize in the Holy Spirit as he chose. This was one of the very first things that repelled me about the Assemblies of God position. I saw it in its historical perspective as an effort to retain human control over the uncontrollable Holy Spirit. (3) Tongues can be counterfeited either through ignorance, religious pressure to conform or even demonic influence. This has led to justified criticism of abuses resulting from our tradition that has devalued the genuine manifestation of spiritual gifts including tongues. (4) My search of Scripture led me to conclude the real purpose of tongues that accompany Spirit baptism is to affirm that every people group, race and language must be accepted into the family of God. It was a sign to everyone bound by cultural bias or racial prejudice that there are no second class citizens in God's kingdom. Allow me the privilege of leading you through the process by which I believe the Holy Spirit led me to this conclusion.

First, carefully consider the initial outpouring of the Holy Spirit upon the 120 disciples on the day of Pentecost. On this popular Jewish holy day, fifty days after Passover, Jews and proselytes (Gentiles converted to Judaism) from all over the Roman Empire had gathered in Jerusalem to celebrate. Thousands of these devout pilgrims were milling about in the temple courtyard when from a nearby house they heard an astounding sound. Listening carefully, each national group represented heard God being extolled in his own language. Soon, the 120 poured out of the house and joined the thousands of pilgrims in the temple courtyard. It was an amazing scene as the disciples continued to worship and praise God in the various languages understood by the assembled throng. Luke graphically describes the scene in Acts 2:5-17

Now there were staying in Jerusalem God-fearing Jews from every nation of the world. When they heard this sound, a crowd came together in bewilderment, because each heard them speaking in his own language. Utterly amazed, they asked: "Are not all these men who are speaking Galileans? Then how is it that each of us hears them in his own native language? Parthians, Medes, etc. (15 nationalities mentioned) We hear them declaring the wonders of God in our own tongues!" Amazed and perplexed, they asked one another, "What does this mean?" Some, however, made fun of them, and said, "They have had too much wine." The Peter stood up with the Eleven, raised his voice and addressed the crowd: "Fellow Jews and all of you who are in Jerusalem let me explain this to you; listen carefully to what I say. These men are not drunk as you suppose. It's only 9 in the morning! No, this is what was spoken by the prophet Joel: 'In the last days,' God says, 'I will pour out my Spirit on all people...And everyone who calls on the name of the Lord will be saved.'" Peter's text from the Prophet Joel is revolutionary and clearly states the purpose for tongues that accompanied the outpouring of the Spirit at Pentecost. The amazing truth that was revealed to me, something I had never before recognized, is this: Peter did not believe, practice nor accept the truth that Joel proclaimed. Before you shout, "Heresy," let me demonstrate from scripture that what I say is the simple truth. Permit me to borrow these words from Peter's introduction to the Pentecost throng: *"Let me explain this to you; listen carefully to what I say."*

I think all will agree that "THIS" of Acts 2:16 refers to the languages supernaturally spoken by the disciples at Pentecost and was an indication or sign that *"WHAT WAS SPOKEN BY THE PROPHET JOEL"* had now been ushered in . And what was it that Joel had predicted would be a reality in the last epoch of God's redemptive plan for humanity? It is summarized in the first and last statements of the quotation from Joel. Note them carefully. *"IN THE LAST DAYS, GOD SAYS, I WILL POUR OUT MY SPIRIT ON ALL PEOPLE ...AND EVERYONE WHO CALLS ON THE NAME OF THE LORD WILL BE SAVED."* (Acts 2:17a & 21). What I was very slow in recognizing is this: Peter, even after Pentecost, was so in bondage to his Jewish tradition that he could not accept or believe that "ALL PEOPLE" were now welcomed to be recipients of the Holy Spirit. Peter was still convinced this was a privilege reserved only for Jews or proselytes. This is clearly revealed in Acts 10. Peter interpreted the "EVERYONE" of verse 21 to mean "any Jew or proselyte..." Despite being baptized in the Spirit, despite three years under the teaching and example of Jesus, despite the clear declaration of the very Old Testament prophet whom he quoted in his sermon text, Peter never understood the significance of the sign of tongues. Tongues were a sign of the universality of the gospel. Until Peter and the other disciples (all Jews) understood and accepted that, the church was "dead in the water."

I can only conjecture how Peter and the other disciples initially interpreted the purpose of tongues. Perhaps they thought, in keeping with their tradition: "Speaking in tongues proves how special we are. Only we have been baptized in the Spirit." As I say, that is only conjecture. However, we do know this; God, through a series of miracles chronicled in Acts 10, finally got through to Peter and he at last was freed from his egoistic, obsessive, biased tradition. The culmination of this miraculous process is described in Acts 10:44-48. You, no doubt, remember Peter had barely started his sermon when he was interrupted by

Jesus, the sovereign Baptizer in the Holy Spirit. Luke describes it this way: *"While Peter was still speaking these words, the Holy Spirit came on all who heard the message. The circumcised believers who had come with Peter were astonished that the gift of the Holy Spirit had been poured out even on the Gentiles. For they heard them speaking in tongues and praising God. Then Peter said, 'Can anyone keep these people from being baptized with water? They have received the Holy Spirit just as we have. So he ordered that they be baptized in the name of Jesus Christ. Then they asked Peter to stay with them for a few days.'"*

Is it not obvious that the sign of tongues spoken by the new Gentile believers was the culmination of the series of signs to Peter that now "ALL PEOPLE" were to be welcomed into the family of God, just as Joel had predicted? The sign of languages spoken by supernatural enablement, when accompanying Spirit baptism, was Christ's reminder that every people group, race, culture and language was welcome to equally participate in his kingdom. Whether the outpouring of the Spirit happened at Caesarea upon Roman soldiers or at Azusa Street in Los Angeles on African Americans a generation out of slavery, the message from Christ was the same; "there are no second class citizens in my kingdom."

Another pertinent Old Testament passage that relates to speaking in tongues is quoted by the apostle Paul in his first letter to the Corinthian church. He counsels this Pentecostal congregation: *"Brothers, stop thinking like children. In regard to evil be infants, but in your thinking be adults. In the law it is written: 'Through men of strange tongues and through the lips of foreigners I will speak to this people, but even then they will not listen to me', says the Lord."* (I Corinthians 14:20-21)

Paul uses this Isaiah passage to undergird a principle he is about to present concerning tongues that accompanied the outpourings of the Spirit at Pentecost and subsequent Spirit baptisms. The principle he presents is this: *"Tongues, then, are a sign, not for believers but for unbelievers."* We can be assured that Paul has the Spirit outpourings at Pentecost and subsequently in view. Why? Because in these events there is en masse speaking in tongues fully approved by Jesus and his apostles. Here, also, there are unbelievers present who fit the pattern established in the Old Testament text from Isaiah. The "unbelievers" are God's chosen people (Jews) who need a dramatic sign to free them from their captivity to a bigoted, biased tradition that will stop the infant church in its tracks. Tongues are a divine signal that every people group, every race, every culture and language are invited to call upon the Lord Jesus and be saved. (Acts 2:21)

As they say, "The proof of the pudding is in the eating." Let's see if this interpretation of Paul's principle extracted from Isaiah 28:11-12 fits when applied to generic tongues. First, consider the initial outpouring of the Spirit at Pentecost. The one hundred twenty obedient disciples were waiting in Jerusalem for the promised Holy Spirit. John the Baptist had predicted of Jesus, *"He will baptize you with the Holy Spirit and fire."* When Jesus baptized these disciples he fulfilled John's prophecy, and "tongues as of fire" rested on each of them. This was the proof, the initial evidence, if you will, that Jesus had baptized them in the Spirit as promised. Tongues were not predicted nor expected. They had no "sign" value to the disciples. Then why tongues? They were a sign to the unbelievers, just as Paul recognized. And who were the Unbelievers? Why, of course, the thousands of Jewish pilgrims gathered from all over the Roman Empire to celebrate the feast of Pentecost in Jerusalem. When they heard unlettered Galilean peasants fluently speaking the languages of Libya, Egypt, Crete, Arabia, etc., they were flabbergasted . Their spiritual antennae were sensitized and they began to question the meaning of this amazing phenomenon.

This gave Peter the opportunity to preach a powerful sermon that resulted in three thousand unbelievers becoming believers.

The next outpouring of the Spirit accompanied by tongues is upon the Roman garrison in Caesarea. Peter has been drafted by the Holy Spirit as a reluctant chaplain to take the gospel to the centurion, Cornelius, and his family, friends, and military associates. Peter is thoroughly immersed in his Jewish tradition which forbids all social contacts with Gentiles. All the Jewish Christians believed Gentiles must submit to Mosaic rites in order to enter the family of God. Among other things, this included circumcision and dietary restrictions. Gentiles would never acquiesce to this. Since the first followers of Jesus were Jews, how was the gospel going to penetrate "to the ends of the earth?" There was only one way this could be accomplished. The racial bias of the Jewish Christians had to be nipped in the bud. If not, the church would be stillborn.

Relive with me one of the most momentous events in Christian history. Peter arrived at Cornelius' quarters accompanied by several Jewish Christians from Joppa. After mutual greetings, Cornelius quickly assembled his family, friends and military associates to hear what Peter had to say. Barely into his sermon, Jesus interrupted Peter and poured out the Holy Spirit upon the assembled throng of Gentiles and they began speaking in tongues. It would be hard to guess who was the most surprised, the Gentiles or Jewish Christians. The report recorded in Acts 10 leads me to believe the Jewish Christians took the surprise prize. Luke writes, *"The uncircumcised believers who had come with Peter were astonished that the gift of the Holy Spirit had been poured out even on the Gentiles. For they heard them speaking in tongues and praising God* (Acts 10:45-46 NIV). The Greek word translated "astonished" is a very strong word expressing consternation and overwhelming amazement. Peter's response was immediate. *"Can anyone keep these people from being baptized with water? They have received the Holy Spirit just as we have. So he ordered that they be baptized in the name of Jesus Christ"* Acts 10:47-48. At last Peter believed what he had preached at Pentecost: *"In the last days, God says, I will pour out my Spirit on all people...and everyone who calls on the name of the Lord will be saved"* Acts 2:17,21.

Consider the historical significance of this episode. Who are the unbelievers for whom the tongues at Caesarea were a sign? It's obvious the sign was for Peter and his brethren from Joppa who did not believe Gentiles could be saved without submitting to Jewish rites. Jesus knew his followers must realize that every nationality, every language, every race and culture were welcome into the fellowship of his kingdom. This is BIG. This is transformational. This is what the sign of tongues accompanying Spirit baptism is all about. This was the purpose at Pentecost, Caesarea and Azusa Street.

To reduce speaking in tongues to individual initial evidence of Spirit baptism discredits its intended purpose. Rather than promoting spiritual unity and mutual acceptance, it often becomes divisive and can (and has) led to a spiritual caste system. I believe when the Church recognizes and proclaims the unifying purpose of tongues accompanying Spirit baptism, Jesus, the Baptizer, will be glorified and the power of the Spirit will be released in unifying grandeur.

Grant it, Lord Jesus, sovereign Baptizer!

eight

THE EXPERIENCE OF BEING BAPTIZED
IN THE HOLY SPIRIT

A good friend, and long-time member of the Assemblies of God, asked me a pertinent question relating to the experience of being baptized in the Holy Spirit. It went something like this, "What sort of manifestation should be expected by believers who are seeking to be baptized in the Holy Spirit that accords with your understanding of speaking in tongues?" I imagine that question resonates with many traditional Pentecostal/charismatic believers.

It is fitting that we joyfully let JESUS, the Baptizer, determine the spiritual manifestations he desires to accompany one's baptism in the Spirit. For decades we Pentecostals have taught that the initial physical evidence is always speaking in tongues. We have assumed that it must be speaking in tongues. That is not a valid assumption for, as the apostle declares *"Tongues, then, are a sign, not for believers, but for unbelievers."* The primary purpose of tongues was and is to promote unity within the body of Christ by giving a physical sign that all language groups are welcome into the family of God. Jesus, the Baptizer, is the sovereign Lord of this baptismal event. We freely and joyfully acknowledge his sovereignty. We do not put him in a box he has not constructed for himself. We surrender to his Lordship. Some may speak in tongues, some may not. But all will experience a fresh power and anointing for service and "character construction."

When three thousand responded to Peter's sermon at Pentecost he assured them they would "receive the gift of the Holy Spirit." Did they all speak in tongues? We don't know but likely not because tongues had already achieved their purpose for this diverse group of Jews and proselytes. But they did all receive power to begin to act like Jesus. They sold possessions to meet needs; they met together for loving fellowship, they lived compassionate, holy lives and brought honor to the cause of Christ. This is the power Christ promised and the power we now seek. This is the evidence that will promote unity and advance God's kingdom.

You will be awed by the Lord's personal involvement in your life. He deals with each one of us uniquely in keeping with our distinct personalities, culture and backgrounds. I discovered this many years ago as a Pentecostal Navy chaplain serving in Iceland. I'll share it with you as it may help some.

CDR. Carl Wilgus was the senior officer in a squadron of Navy Super Constellations that deployed to Keflavik Naval Air Station when I was stationed there in 1964-66. Carl was an outstanding naval officer and commander. But more than that, he was a stalwart charismatic Christian of impeccable moral character. His life so impacted younger pilots under his command that some became Christians. One such pilot was Bob Wright, who, by his own testimony, was a nominal Lutheran but had never been born again. He was led to Christ and became an enthusiastic follower of Jesus. However, he quickly became aware that he needed more power in his life to represent Jesus adequately. One of his charismatic friends witnessed to him about the baptism in the Holy Spirit and recommended he talk to the Pentecostal chaplain about this experience.

We met and talked and Bob said he wanted to pray to be filled with the Spirit. I agreed to pray with him and so the two of us met in the chapel annex. I encouraged him to concentrate on worshipping Jesus and to thank him for salvation and the promise of his Spirit. Bob prayed but very quietly. Honestly, I didn't sense that much was going on. I didn't see any outward manifestation that God was doing anything significant in his life. It was late at night and I was ready to give up and go home. But Bob just kept on earnestly praying, barely moving his lips. So I persevered and stayed, and stayed, and stayed. At last Bob concluded his talk with God.

What a talk it must have been! He had prayed like a Lutheran, not like a Pentecostal, but he touched God. He testified that there had been a dynamic encounter with the Baptizer. Jesus had flooded his consciousness with the wonder of his presence and he knew he had been baptized in the Holy Spirit. And I thought nothing was happening! His life was transformed and empowered although there had been no speaking in tongues during this experience. Bob said that some time later he did receive the gift of tongues although it did not accompany his Spirit baptism. This gift, however, has richly blessed his devotional life.

After retiring from the Navy, Bob and his wife, Mary Jane, were called into full time ministry of church planting. They established or assisted in establishing eight new churches. Providentially, we met again thirty years later in 1996. He has accompanied me to Ukraine and Hungary several times as well as going on his own. The fruit from his Spirit baptism continues now more than forty years later.

Yes, God deals with us individually. He knows us, he loves us, and he has a plan for each life. He wants to baptize you in the Holy Spirit to empower you, to gift you, and to enable you to become more like Jesus Christ. He will decide the manifestation of the Spirit that is appropriate for you and your situation. He may flood your soul with such love that you want to embrace the world. Or he may electrify you with overflowing joy that fills your heart with glorious song. Or he may lead you to speak out in a language he provides. Or you may experience all of these or something else that he tailors just for you.

"Tailor" is a fitting word. Jesus told his disciples just before his ascension, "I am going to send you what my Father has promised: but stay in the city until you have been clothed with power from on high." Luke 24:49 NIV. Jesus is the master "Tailor" who clothes us with the Holy Spirit. He does not provide a "one size fits all" garment. He takes into consideration all our "measurements"...our personality, our strengths, our weaknesses, our culture, genetic and environmental factors. We can't all wear identical clothes nor does Jesus baptize everyone in the Holy Spirit in the same fashion. But you can be assured of this, he has a purpose and plan for your life that takes everything about you into consideration. He will see to it that you are properly dressed for the occasion.

Jesus is the Baptizer and you can trust him. The experience of being baptized in the Holy Spirit will be a wonderful, transforming encounter between you and Jesus as he empowers you with the same Spirit that empowered him. Let every hungry, thirsty candidate for baptism in the Holy Spirit come into His Presence. Jesus is waiting to baptize and empower you.

nine

INDOCTRINATION, A SUBSTITUTE
FOR BIBLICAL TRUTH

I committed my life to Jesus Christ over sixty years ago as a young soldier. I told Jesus that I could not possibly serve Him unless He baptized me in the Holy Spirit and provided the power He promised to His followers. Jesus and I had a dynamic dialogue in which He confronted me with issues that had to be resolved. When we had resolved the issues and my commitment was clear of any reservations He poured out His Spirit upon me. This experience culminated in me worshipping the Lord in a language the Spirit provided.

Because of years of indoctrination in the Assemblies of God tradition I assumed that speaking in tongues was the evidential proof that I had been baptized in the Spirit. I was grateful for the experience and I never doubted the reality of the gift of tongues. However, I knew deep in my heart that proof of baptism in the Spirit for me personally was spiritual power and not tongues. However, there are many who had an experience similar to mine who believe this experience validates the Assemblies of God tradition concerning tongues and Spirit baptism. These people apparently never ask the question: "Is there a more Scriptural explanation for tongues that may accompany

Spirit baptism?" Since the question is not asked an answer is not sought. And millions accept the assumption which fragments the body of Christ and claim it to be a biblical doctrine.

When I ask, "Will you show me the Scripture that undergirds your belief?" they refer to the outpourings of the Spirit in Jerusalem (Pentecost, on Jews and proselytes), Caesarea (European Gentiles, Roman soldiers), and Ephesus (Asian Gentiles). What happened on these occasions is obvious. Those baptized in the Spirit spoke in tongues. But the purpose was to not to give evidence of Spirit baptism. The tongues were a sign that every language, every nation, every race, every people group was now welcome into the kingdom of God.

Thousands of pilgrims celebrating Pentecost asked what was the meaning of the tongues spoken by the 120. Peter's answer was to quote the prophet Joel. "This" (tongues) called attention to Joel's "that." *'I will pour out my Spirit upon ALL humanity'*. No longer was God's Spirit limited to Jews. The various tongues are a dramatic representation of "all humanity" and the universality of the gospel.

Many Pentecostals are hesitant to reexamine Scripture and history lest they discover a refutation of their hallowed tradition. My observation of theological training within American Pentecostal institutions is that too often it is indoctrination rather than education. (Someone I trust said this was not true at the Assemblies of God Theological Seminary. It may not have been true under previous leadership but I have reason to believe it is today.)

I was asked by a professor of pastoral theology at one of the Assemblies of God universities if I would speak to his students about ministering in our armed forces as a military chaplain. I agreed to do so. I then offered to provide each of his students a copy of *Pentecost REVISITED* which relates some of my chaplaincy experiences. But it also deals with my opposition to the Assemblies of God tradition of the purpose of tongues that accompanies Spirit baptism. The professor did not respond to my offer. Was he fearful of exposing his students to an examination of Scripture that did not support his indoctrination? I think so.

Furthermore, Pentecostals persist in insisting that tongues must accompany every valid Spirit baptism because their distinctive identity is hinged to this tradition. Tradition is more difficult to break away from than doctrine. Why is this true? For Evangelical Christians doctrine (hopefully) must be based on the clear teaching of Scripture. If there is disagreement about a particular doctrine there is a common agreed upon authority that can be researched and investigated. This is not true of tradition. It is based upon experiences (or lack thereof), dogmatic assertions by influential leaders, anecdotal illustrations, and assumptions based largely on isolated texts divorced from the whole context of Scripture. This is true of traditional Pentecostal teaching on tongues as well as Cessationism's tradition that tongues ended when the apostles died or when the canon of Scripture was sealed. When tradition is adopted as a "fundamental truth" this "distinctive" must be protected at all costs. The egos of those in leadership are heavily involved so that any threat to the tradition is taken as a personal threat.

Despite the obstacles to change, I know the Holy Spirit is at work to align Pentecostal tradition with Scriptural truth. There is an undercurrent of hunger for life changing, church transforming spiritual power devoid of superficiality. This hunger will not be satisfied by initial evidence that can be counterfeited, manipulated and abused. There is a hunger for doctrinal truth that unites the body of Christ instead of a traditional distinctive that fragments the Lord's body. Where are the leaders who will ignite this spiritual hunger into a burning desire for unity firmly founded in truth? I believe God will raise them up when the Church is ready to respond. Lord, speed the day.

ten

AN AMAZING TRUTH

After I made public my disagreement with my church regarding their position on tongues relating to being filled with the Holy Spirit I was privy to some interesting conversations. I discovered, what was to me, an amazing truth about the denomination to which I belonged for more than half a century. Some clergy do not believe the "fundamental truth" about evidential tongues to which they assert their allegiance. They recognize the lack of a scriptural foundation for affirming that there can be no valid baptism in the Holy Spirit unless evidenced by the initial sign of speaking in tongues. There are multitudes of testimonies, both past and present, in which Spirit-filled men and women who have not spoken in tongues have ministered powerfully through the gifts the Holy Spirit has bestowed upon them. This has and continues to include miraculous "signs and wonders" even though speaking in tongues is not one of them. Many Pentecostals know these things to be true and yet they continue to affirm allegiance to a divisive doctrine without biblical support. Why?

I have listened as different explanations are given for their dissembling. One common denominator for "not rocking the boat" is that to do so would threaten the very existence of the denomination. In some eyes it's more important to maintain the religious bureaucracy than to maintain integrity and truth. I don't think it would threaten the denomination's life. Rather, I think it would provide an infusion of new life into Pentecostalism around the world. Tongues are not the problem. It is the invalid purpose which has been assigned them that is so destructive to unity in Christ.

Another explanation that sounds religious and spiritual goes like this. "If we acknowledged that we have erred about the purpose of tongues it will discourage people from seeking to be filled with the Holy Spirit." Not so. Not so. Rather, it will be the prelude to a mighty, universal outpouring of the Spirit void of the superficial and counterfeit. Jesus reads hearts, not lips. Jesus read the hearts of the Roman soldiers at Caesarea and poured out His Spirit upon them to the consternation of Jewish Christian observers led by Peter. The Pentecostal experience of the Gentiles was evidence to the befuddled onlookers that their theology was out of touch with God's reality.

Once the church turns the mechanics of being baptized in the Spirit back to the sovereign Baptizer, Spirit baptisms will multiply. Freed from the fear of Pentecostal extremism, the empowering experience of being filled with the Spirit will be eagerly pursued. I am thoroughly convinced of this because I have seen signs of its truth.

We Pentecostals have pointed with pride to our supernatural experience of speaking in tongues. We have claimed that it is evidence of a higher level of spirituality than those who have not had such an experience as verification of Spirit baptism. The apostle Paul learned the painful lesson that spiritual experiences, no matter how elevated and heavenly, were no measure of godly power or Christian character. More frightening, even genuine supernatural experiences can lead to pride and a spiritual caste system. God painfully reminded the great Apostle of this dangerous possibility with a painful "thorn in his flesh." What will be God's disciplinary action against us Pentecostals? Is it the fragmentation that has become so prevalent?

eleven

THE TENACIOUS HOLDING POWER
OF RELIGIOUS TRADITION

When I talk to my Assemblies of God friends the reason I hear most often for tenaciously holding to their tradition is this: "That's how I experienced the baptism in the Holy Spirit so it must be true. Would God let me experience something that was false?" The experience may be genuine. It is the unscriptural purpose assigned to the valid experience that is untrue. Tongues absolutely accompanied the outpouring of the Spirit at Pentecost, Caesarea and Ephesus. No Bible student can deny this. Tongues still accompany some Spirit baptisms today as they did mine. But as Joel points out, the tongues are a sign that the gospel and the Spirit are now available to every language, every nationality and race without distinction or limitation. All are equally welcome to participate in God's kingdom. Unknown tongues (to the speaker) are a powerful symbol of the universality of the New Covenant that was ushered in at Pentecost.

Another troubling aspect of the traditional Pentecostal position on Spirit baptism and speaking in tongues is the history of how this tradition was introduced. I am indebted for much of what follows to Dr. Edith Blumhofer, noted Pentecostal historian and author of *THE ASSEMBLIES OF GOD*. I particularly want to discuss two historical insights noted by Blumhofer: (1) The character of Charles Parham, originator of the tradition and (2) The tactics used by supporters to assure adoption of the tradition.

Charles Parham was a charismatic preacher, evangelist and educator who ministered in the late 19th century and early 20th. It was Parham who concluded that "speaking in tongues was "biblical evidence" for the baptism with the Holy Spirit". Blumhofer suggests that there is reason for giving credence to the view that Parham "had purposely created a setting in which others would reach the same conclusion under circumstances in which it would seem to be 'revealed'." In other words, there is evidence that Parham "stacked the deck" with his students to get the result he had already decided he wanted. (Blumhofer; *THE ASSEMBLIES OF GOD*, p.83-84)

As I studied the life of Parham a couple of significant facts were revealed. First, Parham was an admitted racist and was strongly offended by the interracial worship he witnessed at Azusa Street. He denounced it in the most "politically incorrect" language imaginable. He was sympathetic to the Klu Klux Klan as well as to British Israelism. Furthermore, Parham was given to invent many unusual interpretations of scripture such as advocating a distinction "between 'created' humanity and 'formed' humanity. (ibid, p.76). Like the apostle Peter at Pentecost, Parham was opposed to accepting the implications of Joel's prophecy, and for a similar reason. Once again, racial and cultural tradition ignored the sign of New Covenant truth.

Another troubling aspect relates to the tactics used by supporters of Parham's position to gain its adoption by the General

Council in 1918. Here is a summary of the pertinent facts as presented by Blumhofer:

(1) F.F. Bosworth was possibly the best known man within the Assemblies of God in 1918. His powerful ministry, his willingness to endure persecution for his Pentecostal witness, his self-effacing nature all combined to make him a renowned and respected figure within Pentecostal ranks. At the founding General Council in 1914 he was appointed to a one year term as an Executive Presbyter. But something bothered Bosworth as he traveled extensively in evangelism. Blumhofer records, "Bosworth became troubled about Pentecostal teaching on the evidence of the baptism with the Holy Spirit. He thought that it promoted a 'gift' instead of the 'Giver', that it tended to result in 'shallow' baptisms, and that it was the source of considerable confusion...He wrote a persuasive tract and began to circulate his views." (ibid, p. 240).

Although firmly committed to the Pentecostal baptism he sadly stated, "Too many had *noise* without the power." He went on to affirm, "I am absolutely certain that many who receive the most powerful baptism for service do not receive the manifestation of speaking in tongues. And I am just as certain...that many who *seemingly* speak in tongues are not, nor never have been, baptized in the Spirit." (ibid, p. 240-41)

(2) Unfortunately for Bosworth, the editor of the *Christian Evangel*, the most influential Pentecostal publication, was committed to the Parham tradition and carefully screened opposing views. The power of the negative press was too much for Bosworth to prevail. Unwilling to continue the struggle, in July 1918 Bosworth typed a letter of resignation in which he stated, "If I had a thousand souls I would not be afraid to risk them

all on the truth of my position that some may receive the fullest baptism in the Spirit without receiving the gift of tongues." (ibid, p.241)

(3) The uncharitable treatment given to Bosworth is scandalous. Blumhofer indicates an influential Pentecostal leader had "intentionally misrepresented Bosworth" and split his congregation. Others harshly criticized him and asserted he had no right to retain his credentials. (ibid, p. 241) Although he lamented the lack of love displayed he quietly withdrew and did not force a showdown.

My heart goes out to this gracious, deeply spiritual, Pentecostal leader. Would to God our church fathers had taken counsel from F. F. Bosworth rather than Charles Parham. The purpose of tongues was totally misconstrued by Parham and then by others who followed his lead. The cessationists quickly pounced upon the inherent weaknesses of the adopted creed. They reveled in the obvious abuses that resulted. The Pentecostals and the cessationists circled their doctrinaire wagons and shot at each other. Each accused the other of building their defining doctrine on supposition and assumption. Both were correct.

For twenty years after Jesus wonderfully baptized me in His Spirit accompanied by speaking in tongues I never questioned my church's tradition concerning the purpose of tongues. I had grown up in a home where the traditional Pentecostal explanation of the purpose of tongues went unquestioned. My father and grandfather on my mother's side had believed and taught that no claim of Spirit baptism was valid unless followed by the initial evidence of speaking in tongues. Who is going to argue with his father and grandfather?

As I matured and began to accept responsibility for searching the scriptures on my own, I made a startling discovery. The tradition that I had accepted as true was built on a series of assumptions rather than the clear teaching of Scripture. Doubts began to formulate as to the validity of our tradition. I wrestled with these doubts for months as to whether I should confess them to my denominational officials. It was no easy decision because to do so could lead to the loss of my ordination credentials which would result in my dismissal from the Navy chaplaincy. But under the nudging of the Holy Spirit I knew I must be honest and confess my objection and leave the results in God's hands. I did this on my annual denominational questionnaire after returning from Vietnam in 1969.

Efforts were made to have me dismissed by my home district officials in Colorado. Providentially, I was invited to transfer into the Northern California and Nevada District where I found a welcome for the next forty years. Once or twice during those forty years I was threatened with dismissal by the national headquarters of my denomination. Thanks to the intervention of beloved District Superintendents I retained my credentials. I should state that during these four decades I only shared my objections with denominational officials and family.

In 2009 I felt a compulsion to go public with my convictions and my book, *Pentecost REVISITED*, is the result. This book was viewed with disfavor by the national officials. The General Superintendent, a godly man who, like Peter, is a powerful preacher and baptized in the Holy Spirit, strongly suggested to my District Superintendent that he no longer approve my retention. I saw the hand-writing on the wall and submitted a letter of resignation. I am now affiliated with Chaplaincy Full Gospel Churches, an ecclesiastical endorsing agency for U.S. military chaplains, hospital chaplains, etc. This organization is thoroughly Pentecostal/Charismatic but does not have a doctrinaire position on speaking in tongues.

For two decades I was in bondage to a strong tradition, taught and demanded by the denomination in which I was reared. I have been blessed immensely by good, Spirit filled men and women committed to this denomination. Friends whom I admire and respect fill its ranks. Why must I, at this stage of life, "rock the boat"? I'll explain, at least in part.

Godly fear forced me to act upon my convictions. Fear that I might suddenly stand in God's presence without having shared the biblical insights that have become vitally real to me. It was this fear while in Vietnam that prompted me to vow to declare my objection to our traditional position when I returned home. I wondered why we could we be so unbending on a position that was built on assumptions and had no solid biblical foundation? How could we be so inflexible on a position that separated brothers mutually committed to the supernatural ministry of the Holy Spirit? How could we be so insistent on a position that made impossible the fulfillment of Christ's "death bed" request to His Father concerning unity among His followers? How could we relentlessly demand loyalty to a creedal statement that was so divisive, so subject to abuse, so readily counterfeited, and so lacking the biblical support that any doctrine demands? Was the power of religious tradition more effective than Scripture? I couldn't accept that. When I saw a scriptural alternative I feared not to grasp it... and share it.

Love forced me to "rock the boat", love for my church and love of truth. I want the best for the church I dedicated more than half a century to. More importantly, God wants the best for this church which was instrumental in introducing the supernatural manifestations of the Holy Spirit back into mainstream Christianity. I firmly believe we have allowed a religious tradition to "hi-jack" our potential for the kingdom of God.

My insights are not Scripture but they are reflections upon Scripture which need to be carefully considered just as the Bereans pondered and discussed Paul's teaching. The District superintendent of the Northern California and Nevada District, although he has not endorsed the position I have expressed, has strongly recommended that his ministers dialogue about the issues I have raised. I quote from his letter which he sent to the District mailing list: "My endorsement of this book is to recognize that we must constantly be willing to examine our core doctrines and to be sure they are rooted in the sound interpretation and application of the Word... So read this book, search the scriptures for yourself, on your knees, let His Holy Spirit fill you fresh, and do not be afraid of dialogue on even different views. We as a Pentecostal fellowship are and remain a people of the Word and the Spirit." Beautifully and boldly stated. Thank you, Brother Jim! My sentiments, exactly. Unfortunately only one responded to this challenge. Read *Pentecost REVISITED* and its follow-up, *Pentecost REKINDLED.* Search the scriptures with an open heart and mind, and be responsive to the Holy Spirit.

twelve

SEEKING GOD'S PRESENCE

Four years ago I published *Pentecost REVISITED* in which I contested the teaching that there is no valid baptism in the Holy Spirit unless initially witnessed by speaking in tongues. This is a central tenet of the Assemblies of God and other Pentecostal groups. I was an ordained minister with the Assemblies of God for more than fifty years. Forty-four years ago while serving as a Navy chaplain in Vietnam I finally acknowledged to God and myself that our doctrine on evidential tongues is not supported by scripture. I pledged to the Lord that when I returned home I would be honest with my church about my conviction.

I was true to my promise. District officials where I was ordained lashed out at me and wanted me to be dismissed. National officials gave me a year's reprieve to reconsider my position before withdrawing ecclesiastical endorsement. Providentially, I was able to transfer to a District that honored my ministry more than my deviation from denominational tradition. For more than forty years I ministered under the auspices of the Northern California/Nevada District while serving as a U.S. Navy chaplain, a pastor and missionary. As long as I was affiliated with the Assemblies of God I did not publicize my doctrinal difference. When I decided to go public with my book

I offered to resign and my resignation was accepted in 2010. I then became affiliated with an ecclesiastical endorsing agency for chaplains called Chaplaincy Full Gospel Churches.

What has prompted me to write a sequel to my first book? (1) I had become convinced the church to which I had dedicated most of my life had a spiritual deformity that needed to be excised by divine surgery. The sharp blade that must perform the operation is the sword of the Spirit, the word of God. I gave myself to diligent study of God's word concerning the purpose of speaking in tongues.

It finally occurred to me the only Bible the first disciples had was the Old Testament. That's where one must find a biblical purpose for tongues. It was the Old Testament prophets that revealed pertinent truths that I had not understood previously. These are explored at length in *Pentecost REKINDLED.*

(2) Feed-back from *Pentecost REVISITED* convinced me that it was necessary for a voice to be raised decrying the erroneous tradition of American Pentecostalism because of the unnecessary pain this caused many sincere Christians hungry for God's presence. I found the scriptural purpose for tongues, clearly depicted by Old Testament prophets Joel and Isaiah, far superior to the divisive purpose my church insisted on. Acceptance of this discovered truth freed me from the subtle sense of my spiritual superiority that contaminates the doctrine I had previously adhered to. (How could I not feel spiritually superior since I had physical evidence of being filled with the Holy Spirit that my brothers and sisters did not have?)

Thank God, I was freed from this insidious contagion that was so cleverly camouflaged by its association with a truth scripture supports. My question is: how long will it take for traditional Pentecostals to break free from a religious tradition that is founded upon an unscriptural interpretation of a valid experience. Speaking in tongues is not the problem. This is one of the diverse gifts of the Holy Spirit. It is the erroneous interpretation of this gift that has brought such discord, such abuse and misuse, such spiritual arrogance and elitism leading to a religious caste system.

There is an undercurrent of deep spiritual hunger within a growing segment of the body of Christ including Pentecostals. There is a longing for God's manifested Presence unsullied by human manipulation or control. This yearning desire is implanted deep in the heart of earnest believers by the Holy Spirit himself. God wants to engulf us with his Presence as He did Isaiah.

God will not, indeed, cannot, manifest himself other than as He is. Do we realize how God's manifested Presence will impact us when we catch a glimpse of His awesome, glorious holiness. "Holy, holy, holy is the Lord God Almighty." In one flashing, insightful moment Isaiah saw his own woeful, unholy condition and despaired. *"Woe is me!" I cried. "I am ruined! For I am a man of unclean lips, and I live among a people of unclean lips, and my eyes have seen the King, the Lord Almighty."* (Isaiah 6:5) We will never see ourselves as we truly are until we see Jesus as He truly is.

Following Isaiah's repentance, a fiery coal from the temple altar touched his lips and he was assured that his guilt was removed and his sin atoned for. He was now prepared to be God's man.

Although there are notable exceptions, too many Pentecostals have elevated evidential tongues to an idolatrous position. Their experience of tongues as evidence of Spirit baptism becomes the highlight of their Christian witness. No matter what negative character traits they display, they are among the spiritually elite as a result of tongues certifying a valid baptism in the Holy Spirit.

This longing for God's Presence will not be satisfied by spiritual experiences, by church programs or talented, entertaining musicians nor carefully crafted sermons. Nothing but the awesome revelation of our crucified Savior, now risen from the dead and exalted as King of kings and Lord of lords, will conquer our spiritual pride and make us fit proclaimers of the gospel. Help us, my Lord.

thirteen

THE PENTECOSTAL TRADITION AND JESUS' PRAYER FOR UNITY

The lack of scriptural support for the Pentecostal tradition relating to evidential tongues cause many Christians to reject it, including many Pentecostal and Charismatic groups. This doctrine creates major division within the body of Christ and comes into conflict with Jesus prayer in John 17.

Nowhere in scripture does heaven and earth come in closer proximity than in Jesus Christ's discourse with his disciples during his final Passover celebration. Here we see all the persons of the Trinity, Father, Son, and Holy Spirit, on display. We gain a glimpse into the relationship that existed between the Father and Son prior to the creation of the space-time universe.

The climax of this remarkable discourse is Jesus's prayer to his Father. The heart of his prayer is contained in this petition: *"I HAVE GIVEN THEM THE GLORY THAT YOU GAVE ME, THAT THEY MAY BE ONE AS WE ARE ONE: I IN THEM AND YOU IN ME. MAY THEY BE BROUGHT TO COMPLETE UNITY TO LET THE WORLD KNOW THAT YOU SENT ME AND HAVE LOVED THEM EVEN AS YOU HAVE LOVED ME."* (John 17:22-23)

You will notice that Jesus included you and me in his prayer: *"I pray also for those who will believe in me through their message, that all of them may be ONE, Father..."* The amazing thing is not just that he prayed that we all may be bound together in unity but a oneness that mirrors the unity within the Trinity of Father, Son and Holy Spirit. In John 16 Jesus speaks of the ministry of the Holy Spirit whom he will send to indwell his disciples. He no doubt astounds the disciples when he says, *"It is for your good that I am going away. Unless I go away the Counselor will not come to you: but if I go, I will send him to you."* (vs. 7) It is the indwelling Holy Spirit who brings the believer into intimate fellowship with other believers (*"that all of them may be one"* vs 21a). It is the same Holy Spirit who unites us with the Father and the Son thus reflecting the unity within the Trinity. (*"That they may be one as we are one"* vs 22b). It is not that we have the unique unity that binds the Father, Son and Holy Spirit into one divine Being. That is reserved for the eternal, transcendent God. But it is a unity orchestrated by the Holy Spirit that enables us to break out of our self-centered nature and reflect God's self-giving love. *"Be completely humble and gentle; be patient, bearing with one another in love. Make every effort to keep the unity of the Spirit through the bond of peace."* (Ephesians 4:2-3)

Since the indwelling Holy Spirit is the divine Agent producing unity I was faced with a dilemma concerning the traditional Pentecostal doctrine of Spirit baptism. My Pentecostal church tradition taught that all valid Spirit baptisms must be accompanied by speaking in tongues. This makes the Holy Spirit the author of division if the Pentecostal tradition is true. My dilemma is this: do I trust the Holy Spirit to promote the unity Jesus prayed for or do I trust my Pentecostal tradition that produces disunity? I chose to distrust my tradition. I knew the Holy

Spirit would never be responsible for hindering the Father from answering His Son's request for unity.

When I first acknowledged my disagreement with this doctrine it was on the basis of three issues: (1) It was a major cause of needless disunity in the body of Christ. How long was God going to permit this hindrance to Jesus' prayer for unity to continue? (2) It was built on a series of assumptions without a solid foundation in scripture. A major doctrine that separates brother from brother, sister from sister, best be solidly based in scripture. (3) It robbed the Baptizer, Jesus Christ, of his sovereignty to baptize as he chose. Power to become witnesses was all he had promised would accompany the outpouring of the Holy Spirit.

I pledged my allegiance to Jesus Christ when he saved me and filled me with the Holy Spirit. I saw this doctrine as an attempt to give a human organization authority to determine valid Spirit baptisms. I considered each of these a sufficient reason for questioning my church's position. I must reiterate, the issue is not about speaking in tongues. The issue is the erroneous and divisive purpose which we Pentecostals assigned to tongues. I am so grateful for the gift of tongues which has blessed my life for many years. I am saddened that the purpose of this sign gift has been demoted. It has been lowered to a level that produces disunity among Christians. Tongues have a far loftier purpose. We Pentecostals need to elevate them to the honorable place given them in Scripture.

Has the Father answered the prayer of his Son? Has the church of Jesus Christ ever experienced the unity that Jesus requested? The answer is clearly "No". My observation of the

Church around the world is that it is sadly fragmented, particularly among Pentecostals.

Some have wondered why I make such a big deal opposing the Pentecostal tradition of making tongues a necessary sign of Spirit baptism. Let me briefly answer. (1) The spiritual unity of the church is a critical issue to Jesus Christ as is clear from his prayer in John 17. The Pentecostal tradition concerning Spirit baptism and tongues is divisive and needs to be confronted. I make a big deal out of opposing the Pentecostal tradition because unity is "a big deal" to Jesus and should be to his followers. (2) I believe the Father is going to answer Jesus' prayer for unity before his Son returns to establish his eternal kingdom. The sooner spiritual unity prevails the sooner our Lord will come again. Peter exhorts God's people to do what can be done to "speed His coming." (2 Peter 3:11b-12)

(3) The truth of scripture must always take priority over tradition. The Pentecostal tradition is built on a series of assumptions without solid support of Scripture. As Joel clearly points out, Pentecostal tongues were given as a sign affirming that every language group, every nation, every race and skin color (all humanity, all flesh) were now eligible to be filled with the Spirit. Individuals from all people groups could now be saved without first converting to Judaism. The Old Covenant was no longer in effect. The New Covenant was ushered in with the symbol of tongues to mark the transition to the universality of the gospel. The "tongues" of ancient Babel brought division to a world in rebellion against God. The tongues of Pentecost were God's sign of unity in Christ that includes all language groups.

fourteen

THE SPIRIT-FILLED EARLY CHURCH

It is hard to overemphasize the hopelessness and despair that pervaded the followers of Jesus following the crucifixion. They had truly believed that Jesus was the Messiah predicted by the prophets. However, their erroneous tradition was so ingrained in them that they could not conceive of anything but an earthly, political kingdom inaugurated by the Messiah. It wasn't that Jesus had not plainly taught them but it never soaked through. What enabled them to recover their confidence and establish the church?

Of course, one was Jesus' totally unexpected resurrection appearances. Again, Jesus had repeatedly spoken of his death and subsequent resurrection but it did not fit into the tradition that they had been thoroughly indoctrinated in. They even ridiculed the women who brought reports of an empty tomb and angelic messengers who said Jesus had risen from the dead. Only when Jesus personally confronted them in his resurrection body were they convinced. Even so, they still persisted in looking for a political, earthly kingdom.

The second was the outpouring of the Spirit. After Jesus' resurrection, His followers, almost all Galileans, left Galilee and gathered in Jerusalem to welcome the Messiah. They expected Him to establish his kingdom soon. He appeared to various groups there during the next 40 days. It was while they were having a meal together that he ordered them not to leave Jerusalem after he ascended but to wait for the Father's promise of the Holy Spirit. It was then they asked the question burning in their minds, *"Lord, is this the time when you are going to restore the kingdom to Israel?"* He dashed their hopes when he bluntly told them that the kingdom's coming was in the Father's hands and He alone would determine the time. He told them to wait until they were empowered by the Holy Spirit and then be his witnesses not only to Judea and Samaria but to the ends of the earth.

Ten days later, at the celebration of the feast of Pentecost, the Holy Spirit was outpoured as Jesus promised. After the Spirit descended, the disciples immediately began supernaturally speaking in languages unknown to them but clearly understood by the thousands of Jewish pilgrims gathered from across the Roman Empire. Mystified by what they heard, the visitors demanded an explanation. By inspiration of the Holy Spirit Peter quoted from Joel, who had predicted many of the events that were transpiring before their eyes. Peter did not comment further about the prophecy of Joel nor explain the purpose of the inspired languages. I have explained why he did not numerous times elsewhere. Instead, he seized the moment to preach about Jesus, their rejected and crucified Messiah.

The dramatic miracle of supernatural speech witnessed by the religious pilgrims caused them to listen attentively as Peter preached an inspired sermon. As a result, three thousand repented and were baptized in water. These new converts became the pioneer congregation of the first Christian Church.

Peter promised them they would receive the Holy Spirit following repentance and water baptism. Was Peter's promise fulfilled? I believe it was. Did they speak in tongues? Apparently not
or it would surely have been mentioned. However, they did give
remarkable evidence of being filled with the Holy Spirit. And
what they did as the first Christian congregation has become
a model for all Spirit-filled local churches to follow. How did
they conduct themselves as a brand new mega church? Luke
describes it this way: *"They devoted themselves to the apostles'
teaching and to the fellowship, to the breaking of bread and to
prayer."(Acts 2:42)*

Luke elaborates further on three of these elements: *"All the
believers were together and had everything in common. Selling
their possessions and goods, they gave to anyone as he had need.
Every day they continued to meet together in the temple courts.
They broke bread in their homes and ate together with glad and
sincere hearts, praising God and enjoying the favor of all the
people. And the Lord added to their number daily those who were
being saved."* (Acts 2:44-47)

What was the remarkable evidence that this congregation
had been filled with the Holy Spirit? Surely it was not the divisive evidence of tongues assumed by Charles Parham a century
ago. Was it not the invigorating, empowering, uniting presence
of the Spirit producing Christ-like lives? Citizens from fifteen
or more disparate nations were transformed into a caring community, demonstrating love for one another in multiple practi-
cal ways. They manifested such sincere joy in their gatherings
that unbelievers daily were attracted and *"added to their number daily"*. Would to God that believers once again display such
evidence of being filled with the Spirit!

fifteen

A DOCTRINE BUILT ON THE SAND OF ASSUMPTIONS

Speaking in tongues was never meant to be the unique initial evidence of the baptism in the Holy Spirit. Among American Pentecostals it has become a hardened tradition supported by an extensive denominational bureaucracy. I shared this dogma for years until I finally realized it was just a hallowed tradition based upon assumptions and not a definitive doctrine of Scripture. A doctrine so divisive should be absolutely, unequivocally taught in Scripture in order to be accepted by Bible believing Christians. One thing we know for sure; this dogma is notoriously divisive. If it is not true, we Pentecostals who advance this tradition must answer to Christ for thwarting the answer to His prayer for unity amongst His followers (John 17). Our tradition, founded on assumptions, has built an impenetrable wall between brothers and that wall must eventually come down.

At three places where the Holy Spirit was outpoured (Jerusalem, Caesarea, and Ephesus) Scripture specifically states that the recipients spoke in tongues. From this fact, most American Pentecostals have drawn the conclusion that God will not baptize in the Spirit without providing the initial physical evidence of tongues. There are two additional instances (Samaria and Saul in Damascus) where nothing is said about speaking in tongues at Spirit baptism. Pentecostals assume that the Samaritans and Saul spoke in tongues when filled with the Spirit. This may or may not be true.

When I was corresponding with General Secretary Joseph Flower he defended his position by pointing out, "It is reasonable to assume that he (Saul) began to speak in tongues when he was first filled with the Spirit." He makes a similar conclusion concerning the Samaritans. Then based on these two assumptions he makes the grandest assumption of all. "No one is validly filled with the Holy Spirit unless authenticated by initially speaking in tongues." So a universal is derived from three facts and three assumptions. In logic this is called an inductive fallacy

Here is a simple example. "I saw three German shepherd dogs in my back yard. I saw two other dogs but couldn't determine their breed. Therefore, all dogs in my back yard were German shepherds." But what if I went on to say, "And if they were not German shepherds then they were not dogs." You would say, "Absurd." Yes, it is absurd to draw conclusions from unproven assumptions, especially when the conclusions have eternal consequences.)

To further illustrate, suppose you are a Pentecostal believer (Tom) defending your position to me. I (Glenn) am a sincere searcher for spiritual truth. You have declared that no one is baptized in the Holy Spirit unless his experience is initially evidenced by speaking in tongues. I ask you for Scriptural proof and the following dialogue takes place between you and me.

Tom: Acts 2, Acts 10 and Acts 19 all speak of groups who are filled with the Spirit. Speaking in tongues is indicated as the initial physical response to this experience by all participants.

Glenn: I certainly agree. But what about those accounts where others are filled with the Spirit but there is no mention of tongues?

Tom: You must be referring to the Samaritans' experience and the apostle Paul's experience. I am glad you brought these up. What is your question?

Glenn: For a doctrine as important as the one we are discussing I want to be assured of the truth. My first question is this: how do you know for certain that the Samaritans and Paul spoke in tongues when they were baptized in the Spirit?

Tom: Well, it is very obvious that they must have done so. They did in the other instances we have discussed. We can safely assume they did so in these two as well.

Glenn: So your conclusion is based on two unproven assumptions. This leads to another question. Is it remotely possible that one or both of your assumptions may not be true?

Tom: No, I don't think it is possible that I am assuming something not true.

Glenn: So you consider yourself free from the possibility of error? It sounds as if you and Peter are equally bound by religious tradition that is based on a weak proof text without the support of the whole context of pertinent Scripture.

Tom: What do you mean? What's Peter got to do with it?

Glenn: Peter was so captive to his Jewish bias that God had to bombard him with a series of supernatural revelations in order to extricate him from bondage to his religious tradition. Later, he still reverted back to his prejudiced tradition and the apostle Paul rebuked him publicly. It was Peter's adherence to tradition that won him an even sterner rebuke from Jesus: "Get behind me, Satan" (Mt. 16:23) So let me ask you another question. What if your assumptions are based on human tradition rather than the clear teaching of Scripture? Would you still be so certain of their reliability?

Tom: I refuse to believe that they are not based on Scripture. I think my assumptions are correct.

Glenn: You think. You assume, in other words, that your assumptions are correct. From where do you obtain your certainty? Are you omniscient?

Tom: Of course not. Only God is omniscient. But I still think my assumptions are true.

Glenn: But don't you see? If I am to believe as you believe, I must have more than your assumption that your assumptions are true. Assuming a conclusion based on assumptions is presumption and I can't accept that as a foundation for my spiritual life. Since you have admitted that you are not omniscient, is it possible, given only the facts of Scripture, that these believers may not have spoken in tongues when they were filled with the Spirit?

Tom: Well, put like that, I suppose it is remotely possible.

Glenn: Are we sure they were filled with the Spirit?

Tom: Absolutely. You can't question the fact that Scripture makes that plain.

Glenn: No, I can't and I don't want to. All I am trying to do is establish a solid scriptural foundation for my spiritual life. Let me ask you another question. You have finally admitted that your assumptions may not be true. But while we are assuming, let's assume they are true. Is there the possibility that tongues may have had a meaning other than the one your tradition assigns?

Tom: What do you mean? I have never even considered that possibility. Explain it to me.

Glenn: There are two significant passages of Scripture that help clarify the purpose of tongues. They both come from the Old Testament, the only Bible the apostles had. The first is Peter's quotation from Joel 2:28-32 in Acts 2:17-21. The second is Paul's reference to Isaiah 28:11-12 in 1 Corinthians 14:20-22. The Holy Spirit inspired Peter to quote Joel in answer to the question from *"God fearing Jews from every nation under heaven."* These cosmopolitan travelers recognized those speaking in their various languages were unschooled Galilean peasants. They knew they were witnessing a supernatural event. Luke records, *"Amazed and perplexed, they asked one another, 'What does this mean?'"* The quotation from Joel is God's answer to their question..

According to Joel, the different languages spoken under the inspiration of the Holy Spirit symbolized the universality of the gospel. Gentiles no longer had to convert to Judaism to become part of God's chosen people. The different languages powerfully symbolized that every nation, every race, every language group and culture were equally candidates for the kingdom of God. Like you, Tom, Peter had difficulty accepting what Joel proclaimed. He was still firmly committed to the ancient tradition of the Jews. Sadly, it took another eight years before he was finally freed from his religious bias.

Paul extracts another clear purpose for tongues from Isaiah. Here is the principle as recorded in 1 Corinthians 14:22a: *"Tongues, then, are a sign, not for believers but for unbelievers."* How could Paul more clearly deny that tongues are intended as a sign or "evidence" to believers. They were designed to signify something to unbelievers.

Tom: Now you have my interest aroused. Can we talk again sometime? I would like to consider the Scriptures you refer to.

Glenn: We certainly can. Bring your Bible and we will search Scripture together

Tom was beginning to see that a theory built upon an inductive fallacy is a poor foundation for a doctrine that separates brother from brother and sister from sister. To declare that God never fills anyone with His Spirit without initially authenticating it with tongues is opposed by Scripture, reason and experience. If it were true, surely God would have clearly revealed it in the context of Scripture. We Pentecostals have tried to confine God to a box He did not construct. He will not stay imprisoned.

sixteen

THANKS TO NORTHERN CALIFORNIA/ NEVADA DISTRICT

Forty-five years ago this month (February, 2014) I was aboard a helicopter carrier (USS Okinawa, LPH-3) anchored off the coast of South Vietnam near Danang. Our ship was awash with a reinforced battalion of Marines, a combat Marine Helicopter Squadron and a highly trained trauma surgical team. The Marines would deploy in-country aboard the embarked helicopters to engage the enemy forces. My "battle station" during combat operations was on the flight deck, standing by to greet wounded Marines flown in from the ongoing battle.

While this physical warfare was raging about me I was engaged in a spiritual struggle.

My conscience was troubled concerning an unresolved issue I was facing with my church. Let me clarify. I was an ordained minister with the Assemblies of God, a large Pentecostal denomination. The issue I was struggling with was a central creed of my church. It was this: *There is no valid baptism in the Holy Spirit unless initially physically evidenced by speaking in tongues.* I could find no support for this doctrine in the context of Scripture. However, I had not yet shared my conviction with

Assemblies of God officials. I determined to do so on my next annual questionnaire.

When I returned from Vietnam I revealed my variance on my 1969 annual Credential Renewal form for ordained ministers. Immediately the officers of my home district (Rocky Mountain) informed me that they were going to recommend that my credentials not be renewed. That meant that my ministry as a chaplain was in jeopardy. Ecclesiastical endorsement by my denomination was an absolute requirement for retention as a Navy chaplain.

Fortunately, the district could only recommend to national headquarters that my credentials be terminated. The national office alone had the authority to rescind them. After consultation with district officials and me, senior national officials decided to allow me a year to reconsider my position before any terminating action was taken.

I was deeply concerned about my future as a chaplain. I was sure God had led me into this ministry. Had I been mistaken? I knew the Rocky Mountain District was determined to continue to insist that my credentials not be renewed. I could do nothing but respond honestly, pray, and leave the results in God's hands

Providentially, an Army chaplain friend introduced me to Joe Gerhart, Superintendent of the Northern California/ Nevada District. After Joe heard my story he happily surprised me with his reply. "Glenn, transfer into our District. We will have no problem with you." God had answered my prayer in an unexpected manner. I was joyously thankful to Superintendent Gerhart and to our mutual Lord.

For forty years Northern California/Nevada District officials continued to recommend my annual credential renewal despite my disavowal of the doctrine referred to. National headquarters continued to issue my credentials in response to the District's recommendation. I continued my chaplaincy ministry until I retired with honor. After I retired District officials urged me to assume the pastorate of a struggling Home Mission church in Pleasanton, California. I agreed to do so and continued serving the Pleasanton church for nearly fourteen years. After resigning from the church I began twenty plus years of ministry in Ukraine. During this time I never revealed my disparate views to other than Assemblies of God officials and family.

In 2009 I wrote my first book, *Pentecost REVISITED*, in which I revealed what I believed was the scriptural purpose of speaking in tongues at Pentecost and subsequently. I offered to resign at that time but Superintendent Jim Braddy asked me not to, insisting my views deserved to be heard. In 2010 General Superintendent George Wood wrote Superintendent Braddy and asked him to stop providing cover for me. I knew then that I must resign and not bring any reproach upon my friend. I submitted a letter of resignation and it was graciously accepted by the General Secretary. Thus ended fifty two years of ordained ministry with the Assemblies of God.

I will be forever grateful to the officers of the Northern California and Nevada District who protected me, provided warm friendship, and extended a strong right hand of fellowship for forty years (1970-2010). To ALL those District Superintendents and officers, from Joe Gerhart to Jim Braddey, who knew my divergence from the "party line", but accepted me warmly, "Thank you." I love you guys.

An especial note of appreciation to Superintendent Don Annas for his strong support of my ministry and my integrity. His letter to General Secretary Joseph Flower in 1991 resulted in continuous credential renewals for another nine years; and to Jim Braddy for his more recent support prior to my resignation. It was a gutsy thing to do in light of my disavowal of a major tenet of the church these men represent.

I have continued to write and expect to have four more books published this year. All but one deal in one way or the other with further clarification and elaboration of issues introduced in *Pentecost REVISITED*. I have written my first novel entitled *THE TRUTH SEEKERS*. At my age, it may well be my legacy. To my friends in the Assemblies of God, don't judge me too harshly. I obeyed my conscience and what I firmly believe has been the leadership of the Holy Spirit into the truth of Scripture. I had no choice but to obey. Eternity is just ahead. See you there.

AUTHOR FEEDBACK FORM

(Please detach and mail to the address below)

( ) I am interested in scheduling Chaplain Brown for a speaking engagement or book signing. Please contact me.

Name_____

Phone_____Email_____

Address_____

Church Affiliation_____

Here is a list of other books by this author:

> Pentecost Revisited
> Pentecost Rekindled (A 2nd edition of Pentecost
> Revisited with much new material)
> The Truth Seekers (Fiction)

SPECIAL ORDER INFORMATION

Autographed copies of any of these books may be obtained at a special price from the author. You may contact him at one of the addresses below:

Email: rglennb@olypen.com | Phone: 360-681-4250

Address: 161 Sanford Ln, Sequim WA 98382